Numismatic and Antiquarian Society of Philadelphia

Proceedings of the Numismatic and Antiquarian Society of Philadelphia

Numismatic and Antiquarian Society of Philadelphia

Proceedings of the Numismatic and Antiquarian Society of Philadelphia

ISBN/EAN: 9783741130069

Manufactured in Europe, USA, Canada, Australia, Japa

Cover: Foto ©Thomas Meinert / pixelio.de

Manufactured and distributed by brebook publishing software
(www.brebook.com)

Numismatic and Antiquarian Society of Philadelphia

Proceedings of the Numismatic and Antiquarian Society of Philadelphia

PROCEEDINGS

OF THE

𝔑𝔲𝔪𝔦𝔰𝔪𝔞𝔱𝔦𝔠 𝔞𝔫𝔡 𝔄𝔫𝔱𝔦𝔮𝔲𝔞𝔯𝔦𝔞𝔫 𝔖𝔬𝔠𝔦𝔢𝔱𝔶

OF PHILADELPHIA,

FROM MAY 4, 1865, TO DECEMBER 31, 1866.

PHILADELPHIA:
PRINTED FOR THE SOCIETY.
1867.

EDITION TWO HUNDRED AND FIFTY COPIES.

HENRY B. ASHMEAD, PRINTER,
Nos. 1102 and 1104 Sansom Street.

PREFACE.

On the first of January, 1858, eight gentlemen, citizens of Philadelphia, who had long felt the want of such an association, organized a society (the first Numismatic Society in America) for the purpose of prosecuting their favorite study in a more systematic and satisfactory manner. The mania for coin collecting was then raging fiercely, and desires had arisen with very many persons to become better acquainted with the science.

A constitution and by-laws were adopted, and meetings were held regularly once a month at the houses of the different members. A charter was obtained from the State of Pennsylvania on the 19th of February, 1858, under which the Society passed quietly along on the even tenor of its existence, until it became evident to the members that the general interest in Numismatics was not sufficient to keep it in a prosperous condition. Accordingly on the 23d of March, 1865, the name was changed to that under which it now exists, and its scope correspondingly enlarged. This change in the nomenclature and objects of the Society, was followed with more or less rapidity by all the junior numismatic societies in the United States and Canada. Soon the Society became able to hire a Hall for a place of meeting, and for the exhibition of its coins and library, and a wonderful and most gratifying increase was made in the roll of membership.

Of those who first instituted the Society, five are still among its members, two have resigned and one has died. The Appendix at the end of the Proceedings of the present volume, will be found to contain obituary notices, more or less succinct, of all of our members deceased between 1858 and 1865.

Nor was the life of the Numismatic Society deficient in results. Valuable papers were read before it from time to time, which may in the hereafter be submitted to the public. Perhaps one of the most important of its actions, was the adoption in September, 1858, of a new scale of measurement for coins and medals, in place of that of Mionnet, which is the one in general use throughout Europe. The divisions of Mionnet's scale are irregular, and apparently arbitrary. Of the printed copies of that scale which chiefly had been in use in this country up to this time, no two could be found exactly alike, while many of them differed very materially in their divisions. After well considering the subject, the Society adopted as its scale the divisions of the inch into sixteenths, such a measure being readily understood and always to be obtained without difficulty. This scale has been generally adopted throughout the United States, and is known as the " American scale."

SCALE OF THE NUMISMATIC SOCIETY OF PHILADELPHIA,

COMMONLY KNOWN AS THE AMERICAN SCALE.

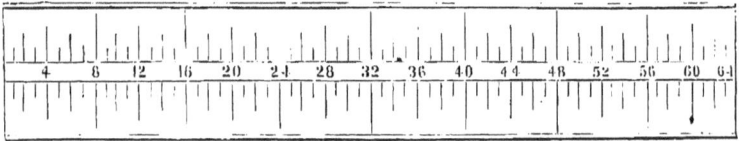

Following the Proceedings in this volume will be found the various papers read before the Society since 1865. It is the desire and intention of the Society to publish annually, at least one volume of Proceedings, and in view of this object, contributions of original papers are solicited from corresponding as well as resident members.

The Society has procured a Photograph Album in which it is desirous of keeping the photographic likenesses of all its members, and the Committee takes this opportunity of urging upon such members, as have not already done so, the importance of sending their carte des visites to the Society.

In the hope and belief that the efforts of the Publication Committee, in carefully issuing these Proceedings, will prove in every way satisfactory to the members, this volume is herewith respectfully submitted.

HENRY PHILLIPS, JR.,
WILLIAM S. VAUX,
ALFRED B. TAYLOR,
Committee of Publication.

MINUTES.

A stated meeting of the Society (the first under its new name), was held this evening, at the house of A. B. Taylor, the following members being present: Joseph J. Mickley, Wm. P. Chandler, Wm. S. Vaux, Henry Phillips, Jr., Emil Cauffman, S. H. Fulton, Edwin W. Lehman, C. K. Warner, and A. B. Taylor.

The minutes of the last meeting were read and adopted.

The proposed amendments to the Constitution were adopted, after being amended by striking out the portion relative to a Board of Directors. In the By-Laws, the proposed new Article, being Art. VI. to Chap. I., was adopted.

A new chapter relative to Standing Committees, after being amended, was adopted as follows: to be Chap. V. Of Standing Committees.

ART. I. The Standing Committees of the Society shall each be composed of three resident members, who shall be elected annually at the stated meeting in December, and shall be as follows:

1. On Numismatics, which Committee shall include a Curator.
2. On Antiquities, which Committee shall include a Curator.
3. On Library, which Committee shall include the Librarian.
4. On Hall.

The Treasurer reported that the expenses attending the amendment of Charter amounted to $31. On motion, an order was directed to be drawn on the Treasurer for that amount.

The Committee on Hall reported that in its opinion it was not only important, but necessary, for the success and prosperity of the Society, that a room should be procured for the

2

transaction of business, and for depositing such donations as are now in possession of or may hereafter belong to the Society. The report was accepted, and the Committee continued, with directions to inquire where and at what cost a suitable hall may be procured, and to report to a stated or special meeting of the Society.

The Committee on altering Plates reported progress.

The following donations were made to the Society:

Three Danish Books on Antiquities, 11 Catalogues of Books, Coins, &c., by A. B. Taylor.

Three Catalogues of Coins, 10 Casts of Gems in Sulphur, by H. Phillips, Jr.

A Card Photograph of Mr. H. Phillips, Jr., by himself.

A Card Photograph of Mr. Jos. J. Mickley, by himself.

The Historical Magazine for April was received.

A very beautiful gold medal was exhibited by Mr. Wm. S. Vaux, being a medal of Queen Anne, bearing date 1710, on the occasion of a Spanish defeat. Its size was 31, and intrinsic value about £5 sterling.

Messrs. Robert C. Davis, Wm. H. Key, and Samuel L. Smedley, having been duly proposed were unanimously elected Resident Members of the Society.

There being no further business, the Secretary read the rough minutes of the meeting, and the Society adjourned.

A. B. TAYLOR,
Secretary.

PHILADELPHIA, *June* 1, 1865.

A stated meeting of the Society was held this evening, at the house of A. B. Taylor. The following members were present: Joseph J. Mickley, Wm. S. Vaux, Henry Phillips, Jr., Wm. P. Chandler, E. Cauffman, C. K. Warner, and A. B. Taylor.

The minutes of the last meeting were read and adopted.

The Committee on Hall reported progress.

The Committee on altering Plates reported progress.

The following donations were made to the Society:

Two Philadelphia Directories, 1858 and 1860, 2 vols. Emporium of Arts and Sciences, and 4 Indian Arrow-heads, by A. B. Taylor.

Two cent piece and one cent piece of 1864 (proofs), by Mr. E. Cauffman.

The Historical Magazine for May was received.

A Paper on the Early Maryland Currency was read by Mr. Henry Phillips, Jr.

A communication was received from Mr. Fitzgerald, Secretary of the Rhode Island Numismatic Association, desiring that a correspondence might be entered into between the two Societies.

A bill was presented by the Secretary in favor of Mr. Ashmead, for printing Circulars for the Society, amounting to $12, which on motion was ordered to be paid.

Application having been made by the Rittenhouse Association for permission to publish the proceedings of the Numismatic Society, on motion, it was

Resolved, That such permission be granted, and a Committee was appointed to prepare the same for publication.

Mr. Hubbard Winslow Bryant, of Portland, Maine, having been duly proposed, was unanimously elected a Corresponding Member of the Society.

Col. John Marshall Brown, of Portland, Maine, having been duly proposed, was unanimously elected a Corresponding Member of the Society.

Propositions Nos. 54 and 55 were read.

The rough minutes of the meeting were read and the Society adjourned.

A. B. TAYLOR,
Secretary.

PHILADELPHIA, *July* 6, 1865.

A stated meeting of the Society was held this evening, at the house of A. B. Taylor. The following members were present: Joseph J. Mickley, Henry Phillips, Jr., Emil Cauffman, Robert C. Davis, and A. B. Taylor.

The minutes of the last meeting were read and adopted.

The Committee on Hall reported progress.

The Committee on altering Plates for Diploma, &c., reported progress.

A bill in favor of H. B. Ashmead for $25, for printing Constitutions was ordered to be paid.

The subject of a new seal for the Society having been discussed, it was resolved to have one prepared. The design for a new one was brought forward by Messrs. Taylor, Fulton and Phillips. The design was adopted, and referred to the three above named members, as a Committee, to have it cut.

A communication from Messrs. H. W. Bryant and J. M. Brown, acknowledging their election as members, and enclosing diploma fees, was read.

The Secretary was authorized to have 500 notices of meetings printed.

The Treasurer was authorized to have 500 bill-heads printed.

The following resolutions were offered by Mr. Henry Phillips, Jr. :

WHEREAS, The seventh day of October, 1865, will close a century since there assembled the first General Congress ever held by the Colonies of North America, whose purport was to resist the oppressions of Great Britain, and to concert measures for the protection of the Colonies and for the repeal of the Stamp Act.

AND WHEREAS, It is peculiarly fitting that the auspicious movement should be celebrated in the city where this germ of liberty afterwards ripened to perfection.

AND WHEREAS, It is peculiarly the duty of the Antiquarian and Numismatic Society of Philadelphia to remove the cloud of years from the memories of great and noble actions, and to trace to their ultimate causes the effects produced in our earlier days, therefore,

Be it resolved, That the Numismatic and Antiquarian Society of Philadelphia will celebrate in a fitting manner the approaching auspicious anniversary.

Resolved, That a Committee of three be appointed to invite a suitable person to deliver before the Society on the 7th of

October next, an oration commemorative of the Stamp Act Congress.

The resolutions were seconded by Mr. A. B. Taylor, and after discussion were lost.

Mr. Henry Ducommun and Dr. C. Percy La Roche having been duly proposed, were unanimously elected Resident Members of the Society.

Propositions Nos. 56, 57 and 58 were read.

The rough minutes of the meeting were read and the Society adjourned.

A. B. TAYLOR,
Secretary.

No notices of meetings were sent out, and no meetings of the Society were held in the months of August and September.

A. B. TAYLOR,
Secretary.

PHILADELPHIA, October 5, 1865.

Pursuant to notice, a stated meeting of the Society was held this evening, at the house of A. B. Taylor. The following members were present: Joseph J. Mickley, Henry Phillips, Jr., Henry Ducommun, Dr. C. Percy La Roche, Wm. H. Key, Emil Cauffman, and A. B. Taylor.

The minutes of the last meeting were read and adopted.

The Committee on altering Diploma, &c., reported that the plates were in the hands of the engraver, and would shortly be finished.

The Committee on Hall reported progress.

The following donations were made to the Society:

Four French medallets, in brass, L. Jewett's Handbook of English Coins, lot of Colonial Notes (about 50), and a Chinese Receipt Book, by Mr. H. Phillips, Jr.

A lot of (7) Catalogues from Mr. Lincoln, of London, through Mr. Jos. J. Mickley.

A Sale Catalogue of Coins for October 16th, by Mr. E. Cogan.

A Sale Catalogue of Autographs, Paper Money, &c., for October 13th, by Mr. Kline.

Six Orations on the Assassination of President Lincoln, by A. B. Taylor.

The Historical Magazine for June and September was received.

Mr. A. B. Taylor exhibited a collection of interesting golden relics (9 in number) from Chiriqui, and read a paper concerning them.

Mr. H. Phillips read some extracts from his forthcoming work on Continental and Colonial Paper Money.

On motion of C. Percy La Roche, a Committee of three was appointed to confer with the Banks of the city and elsewhere in reference to procuring specimens of their notes for the Society.

The Chairman appointed Dr. La Roche, A. B. Taylor and H. Phillips, Jr., as the Committee.

Mr. Wm. H. Welsh, Mr. Charles H. Hart and Mr. Frederick Gutekunst having been duly proposed, were unanimously elected Resident Members of the Society.

Propositions Nos. 59, 60, 61 and 62 were read.

The rough minutes of the meeting were read and the Society adjourned.

A. B. TAYLOR,
Secretary.

PHILADELPHIA, *November* 2, 1865.

Pursuant to notice, a stated meeting of the Society was held this evening, at the house of Mr. Joseph J. Mickley. The following members were present: Joseph J. Mickley, William P. Chandler, Dr. C. Percy La Roche, Henry Phillips, Jr., and A. B. Taylor.

The minutes of the last meeting were read and adopted.

The Committee on Diploma Plate, &c., reported progress.

The Hall Committtee reported progress.

The following donations were made to the Society:

A History of the First Troop Philadelphia City Cavalry, published in Philadelphia in 1815, and a copy of the New York Doubloon, 1787, in copper, by Mr. Henry Phillips, Jr.

A Descriptive Catalogue of Proclamation Medals of the Spanish Kings, in Spanish, published in Havana, 1863. Presented by Nestor Ponce de Leon, Esq., of Havana.

The following proposition to amend the By-laws was offered in writing by Mr. H. Phillips, Jr.:

It is proposed to amend Article II., Chapter III., of the By-laws, by changing the word "three" to "five," and by striking out from the same Article the following paragraph, viz.: "Any members elected during the year shall pay at the rate of twenty-five cents for each month until the first of January next succeeding their election." Also, in Article III. of the same Chapter, by changing the word "twenty-five" to "fifty;" thus changing the annual contribution from three to five dollars, and the contribution for life membership from twenty-five to fifty dollars.

On motion of the Secretary, a Committee was appointed to nominate Officers and Committees for the ensuing year, to report at the next meeting. A. B. Taylor, Dr. C. Percy La Roche and Wm. P. Chandler were appointed the Committee.

Nestor Ponce de Leon, Esq., of Havana, having been duly proposed, was unanimously elected Foreign Corresponding Member of the Society.

Father Pietro Folchi, of Rome, having been duly proposed, was unanimously elected Foreign Corresponding Member of the Society.

Chevalier Jean Baptiste Rossi, of Rome, having been duly proposed, was unanimously elected Honorary Member of the Society.

Mr. Hamilton Creighton, of Philadelphia, having been duly proposed, was unanimously elected a Resident Member of the Society.

Proposition No. 63 was read.

The rough minutes of the meeting were read and the Society adjourned.

A. B. TAYLOR,
Secretary.

PHILADELPHIA, *December* 7, 1865.

A stated meeting of the Society was held this evening, at the house of Mr. Wm. P. Chandler. The following members were present: Joseph J. Mickley, Wm. P. Chandler, Wm. S. Vaux, Henry Phillips, Jr., Dr. C. Percy La Roche, Charles H. Hart and A. B. Taylor.

The minutes of the last meeting were read and adopted.

The Committee on altering Diploma Plate, &c., reported progress.

The Committee on Hall reported progress.

The Committee to confer with the Banks, &c., reported progress.

The amendments to the By-laws proposed at the last meeting were adopted, changing the annual contribution from three to five dollars, and the contribution for life membership from twenty-five to fifty dollars; and striking out the paragraph "any members elected during the year shall pay at the rate of twenty-five cents for each month until the first of January next succeeding their election."

The following donations were made to the Society:

A lot of miscellaneous Catalogues, 2 Coin Chart Manuals, and 2 Stamp Collectors Manuals, 1st and 2d editions, by Mr. H. Phillips, Jr.

The Committee appointed to nominate Officers and Committees for the Society for the ensuing year reported the following nominations:

President—Joseph J. Mickley.
Vice-Presidents—Wm. P. Chandler and Wm. S. Vaux.
Recording Secretary—A. B. Taylor.
Corresponding Secretary—Charles H. Hart.
Treasurer—Henry Phillips, Jr.
Historiographer—Wm. H. Welsh.

Curator of Numismatics—Wm. S. Vaux.
Curator of Antiquities—Robert C. Davis.
Librarian—Wm. J. Jenks.
Committee on Hall—Joseph J. Mickley, A. B. Taylor and H. Phillips, Jr.
Committee on Numismatics—Wm. S. Vaux, Emil Cauffman and Wm. II. Key.
Committee on Antiquities—R. C. Davis, Dr. C. Percy La Roche and II. Ducommun.
Committee on Library—Wm. J. Jenks, II. Creighton and S. II. Fulton.

The Committee recommended the following change in the By-laws, viz.: It proposes the insertion of a new Article, to be Article VIII. of Chapter II. of the By-laws; the present Article VIII. to be Article IX., and the present Article IX. to be Article X. The new Article VIII. to read as follows: Any such person as shall in the opinion of the Society merit that distinction, may, on the recommendation of three members be proposed, in writing, as a candidate for Honorary Vice-Presidency at one stated meeting and be balloted for at the next stated meeting, when a unanimous vote shall be necessary to an election. And in accordance with the above Article, the Committee proposes the following candidates for Honorary Vice-Presidency, viz.:

John Marshall Brown, of Maine; Hon. Stephen D. Bell, of New Hampshire; Hon. Robert C. Winthrop, of Massachusetts; Hon. John Carter Brown, of Rhode Island; Hon. William A. Buckingham, of Connecticut; J. Carson Brevoort, of New York; Hon. Richard S. Field, of New Jersey; Hon. Willard Hall, of Delaware; Hon. Reverdy Johnson, of Maryland; Hon. Lewis Cass, of Michigan; Dr. Robert W. Gibbes, of South Carolina.

The Committee also recommended the postponement of the election of two other Vice-Presidents until the next stated meeting.

A. B. TAYLOR,
C. PERCY LA ROCHE, } *Committee.*
WM. P. CHANDLER,

The report of the Committee was on motion accepted, its recommendations approved, and the Committee discharged.

An election was ordered, when all the Officers and Committees nominated by the Committee as above were unanimously elected for the ensuing year.

Mr. Wm. Duane having been duly proposed, was unanimously elected a Resident Member of the Society.

Propositions Nos. 64 and 65 were read.

The rough minutes of the meeting were read and the Society adjourned.

A. B. TAYLOR,
Secretary.

PHILADELPHIA, *January* 4, 1866.

A stated meeting of the Society was held this evening, at the house of A. B.· Taylor. The following members were present: Joseph J. Mickley, Wm. P. Chandler, H. Phillips, Jr., Henry Ducommun, Robt. C: Davis, Wm. H. Key, Wm. Duâne, Charles K. Warner and A. B. Taylor.

The minutes of the last meeting were read and adopted.

The Committee on Diploma Plate reported that the plate had been altered, and that it was disappointed in not being able to exhibit a proof impression from it to the Society, as one had been promised by the printer.

On motion the Committee was authorized to have 250 impressions printed, provided the corrections were satisfactory to the Committee.

The Committee on Hall reported progress.

The Committee to confer with the Banks reported that it had had printed 250 circulars, a copy of which was laid before the Society.

To the President and Directors of the

GENTLEMEN:—At a stated meeting of the Numismatic and Antiquarian Society of Philadelphia, held October 5, 1865, the following resolution was unanimously adopted:

"That a Committee be appointed to confer with the Banks of this city and elsewhere, in reference to procuring specimens of their notes for the Cabinets of the Society."

In compliance with the above, the undersigned beg leave to address you on the subject, for the purpose of soliciting from you, as a donation, a specimen of each denomination of notes issued by your institution prior to its becoming a National Bank, and which have been retired from circulation.

Hoping that it may be in your power to accede to the wishes of the Society, we have the honor to remain

Your obedient servants,

C. PERCY LA ROCHE, No. 1344 Spruce St.,
H. PHILLIPS, JR., No. 524 Walnut Street, } *Committee.*
A. B. TAYLOR, No. 1015 Chestnut Street,

PHILADELPHIA, *January* 1, 1866.

The amendments to the By-laws proposed at the last meeting were unanimously adopted.

The candidates for Vice-Presidency proposed at the last meeting were all unanimously elected.

The election of additional Resident Vice-Presidents was postponed until February.

The following donations were made to the Society:

United States Mint Reports for the years 1859, 1860, 1863, 1864 and 1865, and Priest's American Antiquities, Albany, 1833. From A. B. Taylor.

A silver coin of 6 groschen, of Rudolph Augustus, of Belgium, 1668, presented by Mr. Clarendon Harris, of Worcester, Mass., through Mr. Charles K. Warner.

Seven white metal Medals, by Mr. Charles K. Warner, viz.:

No. 1. Size, 32. *Obv.* In commemoration of the grand parade of the Philad. Fire Dept. Oct. 16, 1865. *Rev.* "In peace Firemen, in war Soldiers."

No. 2. Size, 32. *Obv.* Abraham Lincoln, 1865. *Rev.* "He is in Glory and the Nation in tears." Born Feb. 12, 1809. Assassinated April 14, 1865.

No. 3. Size, 24. *Obv.* "Maj. Gen. G. K. Warren, 1864." *Rev.* "Commander of the 5th Corps, Army of the Potomac."

No. 4. Size, 24. *Obv.* "Pennsylvania Volunteers, Gettysburg, July 3, 1863." *Rev.* "Bull Run, Cedar Mt., Chancellorville, Fredericksburg, Antietam, Mechanicsville, Gaines' Mill, Glenndale, Chattanooga, Lookout Mtn."

No. 5. Size, 18. "Abraham Lincoln, Presdt. of the U. S., 1864." *Rev.* "The Union must and shall be preserved."

No. 6. Size, 18. *Obv.* "Lieut. Gen. U. S. Grant." *Rev.* Surrender of Gen. Lee to Gen. Grant April 9, 1865.

No. 7. Size, 16. *Obv.* "Abraham Lincoln, 1864." *Rev.* "First Battalion Union Campaign Club."

A series of lithograph notes of various Boston banks, being portions of a Bank Note Detector. Also, sheets of printed names of Roman Emperors, for labelling coins. From Mr. II. Phillips, Jr.

A newspaper was received from Montreal, announcing the names of the officers of the Numismatic Society of Montreal for 1866.

The Treasurer's Report was presented, accepted, and referred to a Committee to audit. A. B. Taylor and Charles K. Warner were appointed the Committee.

A letter was received from Mr. Charles H. Hart, accepting his election as Corresponding Secretary of the Society.

The following communication was read, and on motion ordered to be entered on the minutes.

Although not called upon at this time to make a report, the Secretary has thought that a brief statement of the progress of the Society from its commencement to the present time would be interesting, and accordingly the following statistics have been gathered from the minutes.

A preliminary meeting to take into consideration the propriety of forming a Numismatic Society, was held on the 28th of December, 1857, on which occasion seven gentlemen were present. It was then resolved to form such a Society, and a meeting was called for January 1, 1858, to organize regularly.

At this meeting eight gentlemen were present; one of those present at the former meeting not being present at this or at any subsequent meeting of the Society, although he became a member, and remained one until December, 1859, when he resigned.

During the year 1858, there were elected sixteen members, making the total number January 1, 1859, twenty-five. During 1859 there were elected thirteen, and one resigned, making on January 1, 1860, thirty-seven. During 1860 there were five elected, and two resigned, making the number forty on the 1st of January, 1861. During this year there were four elected, one died, and one resigned, making forty-two on January 1, 1862. During 1862 two were elected, making forty-four January 1, 1863. During 1863 two were elected, two died (Dr. M. W. Collet and Richard W. Davids),* having both been

---

* A short biographical sketch of deceased members will be found in the Appendix.

killed in battle, one resigned, and six were dropped from the roll, they having failed to complete their membership by signing the constitution—thus reducing the number of members January 1, 1864, to thirty-seven, which was just the number January 1, 1860. During 1864 one was elected and one died, the number still remaining thirty-seven. During the last year there have been elected nineteen members, while one has been dropped from the roll, making our present number fifty-five.

Of this number one is an Honorary Member; five are Foreign Corresponding Members; sixteen are Corresponding Members, one of them being a lady; and the remaining thirty-three are Resident Members.

In addition to this number, the Director of the U S. Mint is "ex-officio" an Honorary Member of the Society.

A. B. TAYLOR,
Secretary.

The name of Prof. James McClune was on motion dropped from the list of members.

George W. Fahnestock having been duly proposed, was unanimously elected a Resident Member.

J. Francis Fisher having been duly proposed, was unanimously elected a Resident Member.

Propositions Nos. 66, 67 and 68 were read.

The rough minutes of the meeting were read and the Society adjourned.

A. B. TAYLOR,
Secretary.

PHILADELPHIA, *February* 1, 1866.

A stated meeting of the Society was held this evening, at the house of Mr. Wm. P. Chandler. The following members were present: Wm. P. Chandler, Wm. S. Vaux, H. Phillips, Jr., Charles H. Hart, Wm. J. Jenks, Frederick Gutekunst, Emil Cauffman, H. Ducommun and A. B. Taylor.

The minutes of the last meeting were read and adopted.

The Committee on Hall reported progress.

The Committee on Diploma reported progress.

The Committee on Banks reported progress.

Mr. Wm. Duane was unanimously elected Vice-President of the Society.

The following donations were made to the Society:

A Paper of Enlistment of a Soldier in the War of 1812, by Mr. H. Phillips, Jr.

A lot of Pamphlets, by Mr. C. H. Hart.

The Historical Magazine for December, 1865.

Letters were received and read to the Society by the Corresponding Secretary from the following gentlemen, acknowledging and accepting their election as Honorary Vice-Presidents of the Society, viz.: Hon. Reverdy Johnson, Hon. Robert C. Winthrop, J. C. Brevoort, Esq., J. Marshall Brown, Esq., and Hon. Wm. A. Buckingham.

A letter was received from Mr. G. W. Fahnestock, accepting his election, and one from J. L. Hodge, Esq., now residing in Washington, desiring to be made a Corresponding Member of the Society.

A bill in favor of the Recording Secretary, for $6 75 was presented and ordered to be paid.

A bill in favor of the Corresponding Secretary, for $11 34 was presented and ordered to be paid.

The Curator of Numismatics was directed to obtain the silver proof set of Coins for 1866.

The Corresponding Secretary was directed to have printed 250 cards, containing names and addresses of the officers of the Society for 1866; also, to have printed 250 notices of election of members.

Wm. T. Taylor, M.D., and Joseph Diver having been duly proposed, were unanimously elected Resident Members.

Hon. George Bancroft having been duly proposed, was unanimously elected an Honorary Member.

Propositions Nos. 69, 70, 71, 72, 73 and 74 were read.

The rough minutes of the meeting were read and the Society adjourned.

A. B. TAYLOR,
Secretary.

PHILADELPHIA, *March* 1, 1866.

A stated meeting of the Society was held this evening, at the house of A. B. Taylor. The following members were present: Joseph J. Mickley, Wm. Duane, H. Phillips, Jr., Charles H. Hart, Wm. T. Taylor, Wm. P. Chandler, R. C. Davis and A. B. Taylor.

The minutes of the last meeting were read and adopted.

The Committee on Diplomas reported progress.

The Committee on Seal reported that the seal for the Society had been engraved at an expense of $15. It also reported that a woodcut had been made of the seal at the expense of $12. These expenses were ordered to be paid.

The Committee on Treasurer's Report reported that it had examined the report and found it correct; there being in his hands on the 1st of January, 1866, certificates of 6 per cent. loan of the City of Philadelphia for $500, and a cash balance of $82 26. Signed, A. B. Taylor and C. K. Warner, Committee. The report was accepted and the Committee discharged.

The Curator of Numismatics reported that he had procured a set of proofs for 1866, in silver, as directed at the last meeting, and the cost ($4) was ordered to be paid.

The following donations were made to the Society:

Butler's Ancient Atlas, a Spanish book, entitled "Manera de Rezar sus Horas, &c. &c.," published in Madrid in 1663. Two volumes of Zelosophic Magazines, all that were published, wanting first number; Gentleman's Magazine for 1736, 2 Directories, 20 War Pamphlets, 10 Catalogues, 15 Miscellaneous Pamphlets, 5 Almanacs, and a book of Union Envelopes, by Mr. H. Phillips, Jr.

A History of the Fort Pillow Massacre, 6 Medals, and the Autographical Bank Note Reporter, published in 1849, by Mr. C. H. Hart.

Reports on Commerce and Navigation for 1860 and 1861, Philadelphia Directory for 1862, and 19 Miscellaneous Pamphlets, by Mr. A. B. Taylor.

A Medal in white metal of Mr. Binney, type founder, of Philadelphia, 1796. *Obv.* Bust of Mr. Binney. *Rev.* A view of Type Foundry. Size of medal, No. 26. From Mr. Duane.

The Corresponding Secretary read a letter from Mr. H. R. Stiles, of New York, Editor of the Historical Magazine, soliciting communications from the Society or from the members individually, for publication in the magazine.

The following letter was read by the Corresponding Secretary:

TREASURY OF THE UNITED STATES, ⎱
WASHINGTON, *February* 7, 1866. ⎰

SIR: I am in receipt of your letter of the 5th instant. It is in contemplation to print and sell, at their par value, sets embracing all the various issues of fractional currency, of the issue of which the public will be notified. I think you will have no difficulty in obtaining the sets of coins you desire from the Director of the Mint; but if that officer declines to accede to your request, your application should be made to the Secretary of the Treasury.

Very respectfully,

F. E. SPINNER,
Treasurer United States.

To CHAS. H. HART, ESQ.,
Corresponding Secretary of the Numismatic Society of Philadelphia, Pa.

The Corresponding Secretary informed the Society that he had received a letter from the American Philosophical Society, announcing that this Society had been placed on their list of correspondents.

The Corresponding Secretary announced that he had received a letter from Dr. H. Bronson, together with a copy of his work on Connecticut Currency, for the Society; also, a copy of John H. Hickox's work on New York Currency, from the author.

A bill for postage in favor of the Corresponding Secretary, for $2 75 was presented and ordered to be paid.

The following proposition to amend the By-laws was read: "We propose to alter Chapter III., Article V. of the By-laws, by striking out all after the words 'Corresponding Members' in the second line." Signed by Henry Phillips, Jr., and A. B. Taylor.

The subject of increasing the interest of the meetings of the Society, by having original papers read by the members, and by having printed a series of questions calculated to stimulate the members to inquiry and research, having been brought forward by Messrs. Phillips and A. B. Taylor, was discussed by the members generally.

On motion the subject was referred to a Committee, consisting of A. B. Taylor, H. Phillips, Jr., and Wm. Duane.

On motion the Corresponding Secretary was authorized to subscribe to the "Historic and Genealogical Register," for the Society, at $3 per annum.

Mr. E. J. Snow having been duly proposed, was elected a Corresponding Member of the Society.

Messrs. Geo. W. Childs, Harry C. Yarrow, M.D., Howard Challen, Wm. B. Dayton and Samuel L. Taylor, having been duly proposed, were elected Resident Members of the Society.

Propositions Nos. 75, 76, 77, 78, 79, 80 and 81, were read.

The rough minutes of the meeting were read and the Society adjourned.

A. B. TAYLOR,
Secretary.

PHILADELPHIA, *March* 17, 1866.

In pursuance of a call by the Committee on Hall, a special meeting of the Society was held this afternoon, at 4 o'clock, at the office of Mr. H. Phillips, Jr., 131 South Fifth Street. The following members were present: Messrs. Duane, Zehnder, Phillips, Key, Davis, Ducommun, W. T. Taylor, Hart, Mickley and A. B. Taylor.

In the absence of the President, Mr. Duane was called to the chair.

The Hall Committee reported that it had found a room, which, in its opinion, was suitable for the Society; and the object of calling this meeting, was that the members might examine the room, which is located at No. 522 Walnut Street, third story, and decide whether they would agree to take it at a rent of $250 per annum.

On motion the Society took a recess, for the purpose of examining the room as aforesaid.

Having re-assembled, it was on motion resolved that the Committee be authorized to rent the room, and to get possession as soon as possible—possession of the same being promised about the beginning of May.

Then on motion adjourned.

A. B. TAYLOR,
Secretary.

————

PHILADELPHIA, April 5, 1866.

A stated meeting of the Society was held this evening, at the house of Mr. William J. Jenks, 1322 Vine Street. The following members were present: Messrs. Mickley, Duane, Zehnder, S. L. Taylor, Phillips, W. J. Jenks, Hart, Chandler and A. B. Taylor.

The minutes of the last stated meeting and also of a special meeting held March 17, 1866, were read and adopted.

The Committee on Diploma reported progress.

The Committee on the subject of Queries reported progress.

The Committee on Hall reported that possession of the room which it was authorized to rent could not be given to the Society, as the present tenant could not be removed for a year; and that in consequence of this condition of affairs, it had secured the refusal of a room in the building No. 524 Walnut Street, Room No. 27, on the third floor, for $150, per annum.

On motion of A. B. Taylor, the Hall Committee was authorized to rent this room for one year.

The Publication Committee reported that, in its opinion, the publication of the minutes of the Numismatic Society as proposed by the Rittenhouse Association would be inexpedient, and therefore recommended that in place of such publication, this Society should publish regularly once or twice a year, a journal of its proceedings.

On motion the report was adopted and the Committee continued.

On motion of Mr. Phillips, the Publication Committee was authorized to commence the publication referred to in said report as soon as sufficient money was subscribed to cover the cost of the first number.

The proposition to amend the By-laws in Chapter III., Article V., by striking out the part requiring the payment of five dollars from Corresponding Members was unanimously adopted.

The following donations were made to the Society:

Two five cent notes (U. S. currency), with the head of Mr. Clark upon them, from Mr. Zehnder.

A three dollar note of the town of Sumter, South Carolina, issued in 1866, from Mr. Phillips.

A volume, entitled "Who's Who," for 1861, 16mo., published in London, 1861, from Dr. La Roche.

Eulogies on Senator Collamer, published in Washington, 1865, from Mr. Hart.

The Corresponding Secretary reported having received the following donations:

From M. P. Simons, photographs of the Grant Medal, of Cromwell's Mask, and of the Fallen Collossus of Thebes.

From Hon. James Ross Snowden the following books: Coins of the U. S. Mint and Coins of the Bible.

From the New York State Library, three volumes of Catalogues.

From the New York Century Club, Eulogies on Wadsworth and Porter.

From A. B. Weymouth, M.D., two Seals.

From the Maine Historical Society, Patterson's Popham Address, 1864.

From the Numismatic Society of Rhode Island, a copy of Constitution.

From Prof. James D. Butler, of Wisconsin, a photograph

of the Westphalia Medal, with a printed description of the same.

From Governor Curtin, Messages, &c.

Mr. Phillips presented to the Society his History of Colonial Paper Currency, &c.

The resignation of Mr. John A. McAllister was presented and on motion accepted.

The following letters were read: from Hon. R. S. Field, acknowledging and accepting his election as Honorary Vice-President of this Society; from the Librarian of the New York State Library, together with Catalogues; from the Secretary of the Treasury relative to Currency; from Prof. Joseph Henry, of the Smithsonian Institution, in reference to their publications; from Governor Curtin, in reference to the Colonial Records and Pennsylvania Archives; from Prof. James D. Butler, of Wisconsin, asking for information respecting the Westphalia Medal, and enclosing a photograph and printed description of the medal.

A paragraph published in the daily papers respecting some recent discoveries in Mexico, induced the Corresponding Secretary to write a letter to the Hon. Secretary of State, asking for information. A reply was received, giving what information was in the possession of the department. Mr. Hart also read an interesting paper on the subject, when, after some discussion, on motion, a Committee was appointed to further investigate the subject. The Chairman appointed Messrs. Hart, Phillips and Duane as the Committee.

A paper, entitled "Some Considerations on the best Method of Extending the Usefulness and Increasing the Efficiency of the Society," was read by Mr. Phillips, and on motion was referred to the Committee on Queries.

The following remarks were offered by Mr. Duane:

Since the last meeting of our Society, the death of Jared Sparks has occurred, and it seems eminently proper for us to express our regret at the loss of one who was so eminent in the field of American History.

Mr. Sparks owed the position which he reached, in a very great degree to his own exertions. Born on a farm in Conneeticut, and spending his earliest years in agricultural labors, he did not enter Harvard University until he had reached his twentieth year. Here he earned his education by his own services for the benefit of the University, according to a system then common there, in Yale College, and perhaps in other Eastern Colleges. Many students thus occupied take high rank as scholars, and such was the case with Mr. Sparks, who graduated with the highest honors. Of this Institution he was afterwards the honored President.

His literary labors are known to you all; as the Editor of the North American Review; of the works of Washington and Franklin; and of a collection of American Biographies of great value. He was one of the earliest laborers in the cause of American History, and a worthy compeer of the distinguished men who have since added honor to our country in this branch of learning. Various Historical Societies throughout the country have thought themselves honored by having his name on the roll of their Honorary Members.

In view of this great loss, I have thought proper to present some resolutions upon the subject to the Society, and submit the following as expressive of the feelings which we all entertain.

Resolved, That we have heard with great regret of the decease of Jared Sparks, who has recently closed a long and useful life, a great part of which was devoted to the assiduous study of American History, the fruit of which has been as profitable to the world as it was honorable to himself.

Resolved, That the increasing interest in the history of our country is greatly owing to his labors in the cause; and his industry and zeal are fit models for those who may succeed him in historical and biographical labors.

These resolutions being seconded by Mr. Chandler, were unanimously adopted.

Mr. Chandler made the following remarks:

It can be but little in my power to add any expressions of feeling for the loss which the Republic of Letters has sustained in the death of Jared Sparks, a man whose long life has been so thoroughly identified with and so honorably conspicuous in America and her antiquities. Whether in the fields of biography or of history, or in the less appreciated but equally valuable scope of action as an editor, his labors have been never ending and untiring, his zeal for learning leading him always into the foremost ranks. Perhaps in the controversial positions which he from time to time assumed, it may not always be in our power entirely to agree with him, but our testimony must be given that it is impossible to withhold from him the meed of praise justly due to his knowledge and critical acquirements, so entirely the result of his own unassisted labors. Whilst America holds her place in the history of nations, the name of Jared Sparks can never be forgotten.

Mr. Phillips, Mr. Hart and Mr. S. L. Taylor followed with appropriate remarks.

Mr. Hart informed the Society that from some conversation he had had with Hon. J. Ross Snowden, he had reason to believe, that if so invited, Mr. Snowden would deliver a lecture before this Society, that would no doubt be interesting, and might at the same time be of advantage to the Society in a pecuniary point of view; the subject of the proposed lecture being "Evidences of Christianity, with some notices of the Coins and Money Terms of the Bible which corroborate its authenticity and credibility."

On motion a Committee was appointed to invite Mr. Snowden to deliver such a lecture. The Chairman appointed Mr. Duane, Mr. Taylor and Mr. Hart, the Committee.

The question having arisen as to whether an ex-Director of the Mint, having become a member of this Society during his term of office, retained his membership afterwards, it was on motion resolved, that this Society understand the proper construction of Article IX. of Chapter II. of the By-laws to be, that the Director of the Mint retains his Honorary Membership after his term of office.

The question having arisen as to whether a person living out of the city could be a Resident Member, it was on motion resolved, that it is the sense of the Society that all persons residing in the State of Pennsylvania, within thirty miles from the city of Philadelphia, are eligible for Resident Membership.

A bill in favor of Irwin & Sartain for $16, for paper and printing Certificates of Membership, was presented and ordered to be paid.

The following proposition to amend the By-laws was offered by Mr. Phillips: It is proposed in Chapter III., Article I. of the By-laws to alter the diploma fee from "half a dollar" to " one dollar."

A number of interesting and valuable medals were exhibited by Mr. Duane, among them were the following:

The Peace Medal (Libertas Americana), in copper, in fine preservation; a Jefferson Medal in white metal, in very fine condition; a Medal of Frederick the Great, in commemoration of the battle of Rosbach, Nov. 1757, in brass; the Sansom Medal—Washington relinquishing the Presidency, 1797.

A number of curious and interesting gold coins were exhibited by Mr. William J. Jenks, most of them being in very excellent condition; among them were a gold Rose Noble of Henry IV.; a Ryal of James I.; a five Shilling piece of James I.; a Medal commemorating the Augsburg Confession, 1530; also, a silver Denier of Charles IX.

Three rare Vermont notes were exhibited by Mr. A. B. Taylor, for 15 pence, 10 shillings and 20 shillings, respectively; they were issued by order of Assembly, Windsor, February, 1781, and in this respect differ from what Mr. Phillips, in his recent work on Paper Currency, describes as the only issue by Vermont, the issue by order of Assembly, Andover, May, 1781.

On motion of Mr. Chandler, seconded by Mr. Zehnder, it was resolved, that the following memorial offered by President Mickley should be sent to Congress, signed by the President and Secretary, and with the seal of the Society attached.

[COPY.]

To the Honorable the Senate and House of Representatives of the United States of America, in Congress assembled:

The petition of the Numismatic and Antiquarian Society of Philadelphia, a corporation created by the Commonwealth of Pennsylvania, for the promotion of Numismatic Science and Antiquarian Research, respectfully showeth:

That in the opinion of the Society, the coinage of the United States might be made of interest and of permanent value, by becoming the repository of events of note, whether civil or military, in the history of the country.

That a long and unmeaning series of coins whose chief variety is a mere difference in date is almost an anomaly, and a retrograde step in civilization. A reference alone, of all other examples, to the series of ancient Roman Coins, will amply prove the correctness of these views. Were all traces of Roman history obliterated, it could be rewritten from the coinage which survives.

The minor details necessary to carry such a plan into successful operation, as for example, to certain classes of coins the allotment of classes of events, as on the National Bank currency, might easily be devised by the wisdom of your assembled bodies.

And your petitioners will ever pray, &c.

The following gentlemen having been duly proposed, were unanimously elected Resident Members of the Society: Messrs. William Idler, Pliny E. Chase, Henry Sylvester and Eli K. Price.

Philip Henry, Earl Stanhope, of London, England, was elected an Honorary Member of the Society.

Propositions Nos. 81, 82, 83, 84, 85, 86, 87, 88, 89, 90, 91, 92, 93, 94, 95, 96, 97, 98, 99 and 100 were read.

The rough minutes of the meeting were read and the Society adjourned.

A. B. Taylor,
Secretary.

Philadelphia, *May* 3, 1866.

A stated meeting of the Society was held this evening, at the Hall of the Society, for the first time. The following members were present: Messrs. Mickley, Duane, Phillips, W. T. Taylor, S. L. Taylor, Sylvester, Dayton, Hart, Chandler, Ducommun and A. B. Taylor.

The minutes of the last meeting were read and adopted.

The Committee on Diploma, Book Plate, &c., reported that the Diploma had been altered according to instructions, and exhibited a copy to the Society. The Committee was continued.

The Committee on Queries reported progress.

The Committee on Mexican Antiquities reported progress.

The Committee appointed to invite Mr. Snowden to deliver a lecture before the Society, reported that the lecture had been delivered according to request before a small but appreciative audience; and that since that time the Committee had addressed a note to Mr. Snowden, of which the following is a copy:

May 2, 1866.

DEAR SIR: On behalf of the Numismatic and Antiquarian Society of Philadelphia, we thank you for your kindness in delivering before us your lecture upon the Coins of the Bible, and ask you for a copy of it, to be preserved by the Society.

Very respectfully, yours, &c.,
WILLIAM DUANE, ⎫
A. B. TAYLOR, ⎬ Committee.
CHARLES H. HART, ⎭

To JAMES ROSS SNOWDEN, ESQ.

To this note the following reply was received:

PHILADELPHIA, May 3, 1866.

GENTLEMEN: I have received with much pleasure your polite note of yesterday, expressing the thanks of your Society in regard to the lecture I had the honor to deliver before it, at the Hall of the University, on the 24th ult.

I cannot refuse to comply with your request to furnish a copy of the lecture for preservation among your papers, but I cannot say when I shall be able to do so.

I am, gentlemen, with the highest respect, your friend and obedient servant,

JAMES ROSS SNOWDEN.

. To William Duane, Esq.,
Alfred B. Taylor, Esq.,
Charles H. Hart, Esq.,
Committee of the Numismatic and Antiquarian Society of Philadelphia.

The proposition to amend the By-laws, changing the diploma fee from fifty cents to one dollar, was adopted.

The following donations to the Society were received:

From Howard Challen, Esq., Washington's Private Diary, New York, 1859.

From Minnesota Historical Society, collections of the Society for 1861 and 1864.

From Charles II. Hart, three pamphlets on the Assassination of President Lincoln; also, The Pennsylvania Pocket Remembrancer, for the year 1814.

From the Smithsonian Institution, the following: Gibbs' Dictionary of Chinook Jargon, 1 vol. 8vo; Gibbs' Comparative Vocabulary, 1 vol. 4to; Lapham's Antiquities of Wisconsin, 1 vol. 4to; Squier's Aboriginal Monuments of New York, 1 vol. 4to; Mayer's Mexican History and Antiquities, 1 vol. 4to; Bowen's Dictionary of Yoruba Language, 1 vol. 4to; Ancient Mining on Lake Superior, 1 vol. 4to.

From Wm. Duane, his Canada and the Continental Congress, 13 vols.

From A. B. Taylor, 6 vols. of Journal of Science and Arts, published in New York, and 21 vols. of Silliman's Journal.

From II. Phillips, Jr., the following books, viz.: Roman Antiquities from Trajan's Column, 8vo., Oxford; Smithsonian Report for 1856; Dissertatio Philologica, 4to, Rome, 1751; Gouge's Fiscal History of Texas, 8vo; News from New England, 1 vol. sm. 4to, 1676; Pierce on the Weather, 12mo, Phila., 1847; Buckingham's Newspaper Reminiscences, 2 vols. 12mo, 1852; Sabine's American Fisheries, 8vo; State of the Rebellion, 8vo, London, 1716; Calendar of New York Colonial Manuscripts, 8vo, Albany, 1864; Rossini's Roman Antiquities, 1 vol. 4to, Amsterdam, 1685; History of Engraving, 12mo, London, 1747; La Liberte Reconquise, 12mo, Paris, 1830; Manual of Cemetery Pere la Chaise, 12mo, Paris, 1828; Knight's Life of Caxton, 16mo, London, 1848; Irving's Roman Antiquities, 16mo, New York, 1831; The Art of Tying a Cravat, 16mo, New York, 1829; lot of Engravings (about 50); lot of Pamphlets (about 150).

From Dr. W. T. Taylor, an Athenian copper coin. *Obv.* Head of Minerva. *Rev.* An Owl. Size, by Mionnet's scale, 8; by American scale, 20. A Japanese Artist's pencil; a curious Japanese business (assignation) card; an English shilling token, in silver, in fine condition; a fourpence of Charles II., and threepence of William and Mary (Maundy money); a 10 Solodi piece of the Neapolitan States (silver).

From Mr. A. C. Kline, two human bones from the Peruvian Pantheon, in Lima, brought over by Dr. Samuel Dutton. These bones are the radius and ulna of the forearm, although evidently not derived from the same person.

The following articles were placed in the Hall, on deposit, by Mr. Phillips, viz.: two cards of stone implements (Indian arrow heads, &c.); Photograph of the Louisiana Ordinance of Secession; two Japanese Idols; the foot of a Mexican Idol (terra cotta); large Indian axe.

The following letters were read to the Society: from Eli K. Price, and William B. Dayton, accepting membership, and George W. Childs, declining membership, but at the same time expressing his interest in the Society, and his willingness to contribute to its success; from Dr. Gibbes, of South Carolina, accepting Honorary Vice-Presidency, and thanking the Society for the honor conferred; from J. S. Homans, publisher of the Banker's Magazine, promising a copy of the volume for the current year when complete; from Prof. Henry, of the Smithsonian Institution, with donations; from Hon. James Harlan, Secretary of the Interior, in reference to "American Archives;" from the Secretary of the Minnesota Historical Society, with publications; from Nestor Ponce de Leon, Esq., of Havana, acknowledging receipt of election of membership, and thanking the Society.

A bill in favor of Corresponding Secretary for $2 64 was presented and ordered to be paid.

The resignation of Mr. John McAllister was presented and accepted.

On motion of A. B. Taylor, the Librarian was requested to furnish a report on the condition of the library at the next meeting.

An interesting communication from Mr. Phillips was read, giving an account of and extracts from a Latin book, entitled "De Ratione et usu dierum criticorum ·opus recens natum, &c. &c." published in Paris, 1555. After reading the paper, Mr. Phillips presented the book to the Society.

Mr. C. H. Hart made the following communication to the Society:

I have the pleasure of exhibiting to the Society the accompanying very interesting revolutionary document.

By his Excellency,
George Washington, Esq.,
General and Commander-in-chief of the Forces of the United States of America.

These are to certify, that the bearer hereof,

James Dennison, soldier

in the *seventh* Massachusetts Regiment, having faithfully served the United States *Five years & five months*—and being enlisted for the war only, is hereby discharged from the American Army.

Given at Head Quarters the 11th June, 1783.

Geo. Washington.

By his Excellency's
Command,
J. Trumbull, Jun. Sec.

Registered in the Books of the Regiment.
Jno. Haskell, adjutant.

Secretary's Office, Boston, Novem. 19, 1802. These certify that Mr. James Dennison, a soldier in the late Continental Army, has received the benefit of the Resolves passed the two branches of the Legislature of this Commonwealth, and this discharge is delivered up by their direction.

John Avery, Secretary.

On the reverse side of the paper appears the following:

Head Quarters, June 11th, 1783.

The within certificate shall not avail the Bearer as a discharge, until the Ratification of the definite Treaty of Peace, previous to which time, and until Proclamation thereof shall be made, he is to be considered as being on Furlough.

George Washington.

James Dennison,
Paid July 28th, 1784.
Presented by Simeon Boiden,
Feby. 22nd, 1802.
Election, $20.

It is a preliminary discharge or rather furlough from the Continental army, issued by the Commander-in-chief, according to a resolution of Congress, passed May 26, 1783, on the recommendation of Washington's letter of the previous 18th of April.

Irving, p. 391, Vol. IV., Life of Washington, says: "The letter which he had written to the President produced a reso-

33

lution in Congress, that the service of the men engaged in the war did not expire until the ratification of the definite articles of peace; but that the Commander-in-chief might grant furloughs to such as he thought proper. * * * * * * * Washington availed himself freely of the permission, furloughs were granted without stint." * * * * The paragraph on the back is in accordance with the above-mentioned resolution. The proclamation which had to be issued before the bearer could avail himself of the discharge, was made on the 18th of the following October, discharging all officers and soldiers absent on furloughs from further service.

This is the only one of these documents I have ever seen or heard of, and do not know of its being preserved in reprint. I imagine very few suppose that Washington with his own hand signed all the immense number of these permits which were given; but from the one before me, it is apparent he did, for the signature is undoubtedly his, and there is no reason why he should have favored Mr. James Dennison more than the host of other worthies who stood by him during the long night of our revolutionary struggle.

The subject of Rules and Regulations for the Hall having been discussed, the following Rules were adopted:

1. The Hall shall be open every Thursday evening from 8 to 10 o'clock, P.M.

2. The officers of the Society and members of the Hall Committee shall have the key of the room.

3. Strangers shall be permitted to visit the Hall when introduced by a member, at any time except during proposition and election of members.

4. A book shall be kept in the Hall for the registration of visitors names.

5. No smoking shall be permitted in the Hall on Thursday evenings.

On motion the Corresponding Secretary was directed to have framed the three photographs presented at the last meeting of the Society.

The following gentlemen having been duly proposed, were unanimously elected Resident Members of the Society, viz.: Maxwell Somerville, Frederick Chase, Richard Ludlow, Arthur M. Burton, J. Grier Ralston, Leonard Myers, Joseph A. Clay, James E. Caldwell and Edmund D. Wakeling.

The following were elected Corresponding Members of the Society, viz.: John Ward Dean, Gulian C. Verplanck, John H. Hickox and Henry Bronson, M.D.

The following were elected Honorary Members, viz.: Emory Washburn, George Ticknor and James Lenox.

Propositions for membership from No. 101 to No. 118 inclusive, were read.

The rough minutes of the meeting were read and the Society adjourned.

A. B. TAYLOR,
Secretary.

PHILADELPHIA, *June* 7, 1866.

A stated meeting of the Society was held this evening, at the room of the Society. The following members were present: Messrs. Mickley, Phillips, Hart, Cauffman, Ralston, Warner, Dayton, W. T. Taylor and A. B. Taylor.

The minutes of the last meeting were read and adopted.

The Committee on Book Plate, &c., reported that the old plate could not very well be altered to suit our new name, and desired to know whether it should have the old one altered or get a new plate. It was on motion directed to procure a a new plate.

The Committee also reported that it had procured a stamp for stamping books, papers, &c., belonging to the Society, and presented a bill for the same amounting to $5, which was ordered to be paid.

The Committee on Mexican Antiquities reported that at the present time it was unable to procure any further information respecting the objects of its appointment, and begged to be discharged. The report was accepted and the Committee discharged.

The Committee appointed to superintend the lecture before the Society, by Col. J. R. Snowden, reported that the amounts due for tickets sold had been collected, and the bills had been paid. Also, that the expenses exceeded the receipts by $18

90, which deficiency was on motion ordered to be paid out of the funds of the Society.

The following donations were made to the Society, viz.:

Photograph pictures of General and Mrs. Washington, by Mr. John McAllister. The pictures are profiles taken from their shadows on a wall, and are stated to be as perfect likenesses as profiles can give.

A photograph picture of Washington, by Mr. Charles H. Hart, from the original in his possession, who gave the following account of it:

"A gentleman some years since purchased at a book-stand in New York, an old volume, on looking through which he found between the leaves, this portrait of Washington; not valuing it very highly, he gave it to Major Burns, of this city, who did not lay much store on it either: one day my friend, J. P. Smith, the eminent miniature painter, saw it at the Major's office, and knowing I was much interested in such things, endeavored to procure it for me, which, after a little coaxing, he succeeded in doing. The artist's name is F. Vallee, 1795. Who he was, I know not, but think likely an officer in the French Army, as many of these men were fine artists, and this is certainly a French picture."

Twenty copper coins, by Dr. William T. Taylor.

A specimen five cent note, and one cent token, issued by Bodine & Brother, Williamstown, Camden county, N. J., in 1856 and 1859, by Mr. Wm. Duane.

The following donations were announced as having been received by the Corresponding Secretary:

From Frederick de Peyster, New York, his "Influence of Libraries," 4to.

From W. H. Ruddiman, Philada. "Proceedings of Legislature on death of President Lincoln."

From Rev. D. C. Millett, Holmesburg, his "History of Parish of St. Thomas, Whitemarsh."

From Charles H. Hart, Manual of Common Council, New York, 1858; Discourse on Nath. Emmons, by Thos. Williams, Boston, 1851; Catalogue of Library, Congress, Washington, 1861; Proceedings of Centennial Anniversary of the Am.

Philosoph. Society; Transactions Am. Phil. Soc., Vol. XI., Part I.; Message and Documents, 1864–5; Reply to Address of Roman Catholics of America, Philada., 1785; 18 pamphlets and 5 book catalogues; a frame containing casts from Antique Gems; Battle of Chattanooga, with map.

From Philadelphia Library, Catalogue of Library Company of Philadelphia.

From H. Phillips, Jr., Catalogue of Penna. State Library; Fisher's National Magazine, 3 vols.; Discourse on W. P. King; Broadside Declaration of War, 1812; Pownall's Administration of the Colonies. Complete set of old Franklin Almanacs, for the years 1860, '61, '62, '63, '64, '65; An Account of Lancaster, Eng., 8vo, Lancaster, 1811; Report of the Secretary of the Treasury U. S. on Weights and Measures, 8vo, 1857; Debates of the General Assembly of Penna., 8vo, Vol. I., 1787; Vol. II. and Vol. IV., 1788; Catalogue of London Exhibition, 4to, 1851; Essaic Critico ad Emilie Probo, 8vo, Palermo, 1818; Reflession Sopra l'antigo Lago del Palier, Palermo, 1843; Patent Office Report, 1857, 8vo; Guide to the Capitol of the United States, 8vo, 1854; Guide to Westminster Abbey, 12mo, London, 1851; Catalogue of New York Exhibition, 1853, 12mo, New York, 1853; five sales Catalogue Autographs, &c.; Description of Royal Colosseum, 8vo, London, 1851; Sketch of Russia in 1817, 8vo, New York, 1817; 14 Silk Badges; 100 Ballads of the War; Envelopes, published from 1861 to '65 (various); Book of German Psalms, Germantown, 1799; a MS. Orderly Book of the War of 1812; MS. Diary of John Pemberton, which was stated to contain interesting matters relative to Revolutionary affairs. On motion, the Corresponding Secretary was directed to address Mr. Price, and inquire whether he would undertake to prepare this manuscript for publication.

Deposited by J. E. Caldwell, an Antique Vase, from Pompeii.

The following letters were received by the Corresponding Secretary and read to the Society: from Hon. Frederick de Peyster, Rev. J. Grier Ralston, Mr. John Ward Dean, acknowledging their election as members; from Earl Stanhope, acknowledging election, and returning thanks for the honor conferred.

Mr. Hart read a private letter from Dr. Allibone, of which the following is a copy:

1816 Spruce Street. }
May 29th, 11:17 P.M., 1866. }

Dear Sir: You will be pleased to know that I this night, at 8:27 P.M. completed the Dictionary which I projected in 1850, and commenced preparing for the press August 6th, 1853.

Faithfully yours,
S. Austin Allibone.

To Charles H. Hart, Esq.

In connection with this letter, it may be of interest to the gentlemen of the Society to learn that the manuscript of the Dictionary, as it is now ready for the press, occupies 19,044 large foolscap pages, and a few pages in quarto. The subjects under the letter S occupy the largest number of manuscript pages, being 2,251, and include 700 Smiths, among whom are 90 John Smiths. The letter W covers 2,008 manuscript pages, which is next longest to S.

Mr. Hart presented the annexed description of the new five cent piece, taken from one of the daily papers.

Of the specimen of the five cent coins submitted to the Secretary of the Treasury on Thursday, the following describes the one selected for issue: *Obverse*, the Union shield resting on the tied arrows, denoting peace, (the flying arrows on the two cent coin indicating war), a wreath of laurels crowning the shield, and above, in circular form, the motto, "In God we trust." *Reverse*, a figure 5 in the centre, encircled by thirteen stars set in rays, "United States of America" above, the word "cents" below.

Mr. Phillips read an extract from Heylin's Cosmography, published in London in 1703, and of which the following is a copy:

"This plantation (New England) has ever pretended to be more free than any of the rest of our western plantations, and will not be governed by Acts of Parliament as the rest are,

4

but have set up a mint of their own (a two shilling piece of this coinage is now before me).''

Mr. Phillips called the attention of the Society to the statement of the author in reference to the "two shilling piece," inquiring if any of the members had heard of such a piece.

After some discussion, it was concluded that the author was most probably mistaken, and had reference to a one shilling piece.

On motion, the Corresponding Secretary was directed to have bound, Hickcox's Work on New York Currency, and Phillips' Work on Continental and Colonial Money.

An original India ink drawing of the Loxley House (in frame), was presented by Mr. S. H. Fulton.

The following articles were deposited in the cabinet of the Society by Mr. Charles H. Hart: one Indian stone spear head; one Indian stone hatchet; one Indian stone pipe; one Indian arrow, complete.

By Mr. H. Phillips: one stone hatchet; one Indian stone adze.

A plaster cast of the head of a Gorilla was presented to the Society by Mr. H. C. Bispham.

Mr. Dayton made a statement, that recently many specimens of Indian arrow-heads, pottery, &c., had been found in New Jersey, near Cooper's Creek, some of which he exhibited and presented to the Society.

On motion, a Committee was appointed to visit the locality and investigate the subject. The chairman appointed Messrs. Dayton, Hart and Phillips, the Committee.

Bills for filling diplomas, amounting to $16 50, were presented and ordered to be paid.

A bill for postage in favor of the Corresponding Secretary, amounting to $2 08, was presented and ordered to be paid.

The bill for subscription to Historical Magazine for 1866 was ordered to be paid.

A bill for printing, amounting to $2 50, was presented by the Treasurer and ordered to be paid.

A bill for framing pictures, amounting to $2 25, was presented and ordered to be paid.

A very beautiful specimen of the Erie Canal Medal, in white metal (proof), was exhibited by Mr. Charles K. Warner.

The Hall Committee was, on motion, directed to have the room of the Society opened on every Thursday evening. ˙

On motion, the Treasurer was authorized to furnish diplomas of the Society to such members of the Numismatic Society as might desire it, upon receipt of the ordinary charge, $1.

The following gentlemen having been duly proposed, were unanimously elected Resident Members of the Society: Horace H. Furness, Rev. D. Washburne, William J. Philips, Turner Hamilton, Charles J. Lukens, John Farnum, R. Shelton Mackenzie, James T. Mitchell, I. Norris, Jr., M.D., Kingston Goddard, M.D., Edward Langton, Abraham Hart and Lewis Stover.

The following gentlemen were duly elected Corresponding Members: Samuel F. Haven, of Massachusetts; W. A. Whitehead, of New Jersey; I. A. Lapham, of Wisconsin; Joseph Henry, of Washington; Francis L. Hawks, D.D., of New York.

Propositions from No. 119 to No. 136 inclusive, were read.

The rough minutes of the meeting were read and the Society adjourned.

A. B. TAYLOR,
Secretary.

PHILADELPHIA, July 5, 1866.

A stated meeting was held this evening, at the Room of the Society. The following members were present: Messrs. Wm. S. Vaux, Wm. Duane, Henry Phillips, Jr., Henry Ducommun, Eli K. Price, Charles H. Hart, Wm. B. Dayton, Joseph A. Clay, and A. B. Taylor.

In the absence of the President, Mr. Vaux, Vice-President, took the chair.

The minutes of the last meeting were read and adopted.

The following donations were made to the Society:

From A. McElroy, Esq., Philada., The Philadelphia City Directory for 1841, '45, '46, '47, '49 and '57.

From the New Jersey Historical Society, Collections of the
N. J. Hist. Society, Vols. II. to VI.; Proceedings of the N. J.
Hist. Society, Vol. I. to IX., and Bishop Doane's Address—
15 volumes.

From Hon. Wm. A. Whitehead, Newark, N. J., his contributions to East Jersey History, and Eastern Boundary of New
Jersey, 2 volumes.

From Dr. Ashbel Woodward, Franklin, Ct., his Life of Gen.
Nathaniel Lyon.

From Hon. I. A. Lapham, Milwaukie, Wis., Addresses on
the dedication of the rooms of the State Historical Society.

From John Ward Dean, Esq., Boston, his Memoir of Rev.
Giles Firmin, and Story of the Embarkation of Cromwell for
New England.

From Dr. C. P. La Roche, Philada., Mudie's National
Medals, 1 vol. quarto, London, 1828, and Lord Castlereagh's
Correspondence, 4 vols. 8vo, London, 1848.

From Henry Phillips, Jr., Resumé de Archaiologie, &c., par
F. Champollion, 2 vols. 12mo, Paris, 1825.

From Charles H. Hart, Bancroft's Eulogy on President
Lincoln; Cresswell's Eulogy on Henry Winter Davis, and
placed on deposit two old Maps of Philadelphia, one published
in 1796 and the other about ten years earlier.

From Eli K. Price, his Photograph.

From A. B. Taylor, Tabular Statement of the U. S. Mint
coinage, and large photograph of Dr. M. W. Collet.

The following letters were received and read to the Society:
from George Ticknor, Emory Washburn, I. A. Lapham, Wil-
liam A. Whitehead, John H. Hickox, Rev. D. Washburne and
James T. Mitchell, acknowedging election; from William A.
Whitehead, Corresponding Secretary New Jersey Historical
Society, with donation of books.

Mr. Charles H. Hart then made the following announcement:

It is my painful duty to announce officially to the Society,
that which is already too well known to its individual members,
the death of our Honorary Vice-President for the State of

Michigan, Hon. Lewis Cass, LL.D. I had hoped to be relieved from this sad task by the presence here this evening of our first Vice-President, Mr. Chandler, an old and warm personal friend of the deceased, but being unable to be with us, he has requested me to offer to the consideration of the Society the following resolutions, which I now do in his name:

Resolved, That this Society has heard with deep regret of the demise of its late Honorary Vice-President for Michigan, Hon. Lewis Cass, who has just been gathered to his fathers, full of years and full of honors, like a shock of corn ripe for the garner.

Resolved, That in the death of this time honored statesman and war-worn hero, this Society has lost one of its most distinguished ornaments, the country a patriot, whose heart ever beat in unison with all her interests, whose aspirations were never disconnected from her advancing glory, and whose labors were always directed to the promotion of the prosperity, welfare and greatness of her people.

Resolved, That the civilized world will mourn for one of the foremost and most influential diplomatists and publicists of the age, whose works in its behalf have in all cases redounded in the most enlarged sense to its advancement and advantage.

Mr. Hart then said: In offering these resolutions a few remarks may not be inappropriate. Gen. Cass is known to the world more in the position of an able publicist than as a man of historical and literary abilities. But he certainly was not chosen to the position of Vice-President of this Society for the former high qualities, and so it may be acceptable to the gentlemen present to hear in a few words his claim to the character of a man of letters.

His first production of a literary nature was "Inquiries respecting the History, Traditions, Languages, &c., of the Indians living within the United States," which was published in the infant town though ancient settlement of Detroit, in 1823. This work was written from his own personal observations made during the preceding eight years, while holding the position of Superintendent of Indian Affairs for the Territories. During his superintendency he suggested the expedition, in which he himself bore a conspicuous part, for exploring the northern shore of Lake Superior and the course of the Upper Mississippi, which was commenced in 1820, and of which we have a full account from the pen of that distinguished Indian scholar, the late Henry Rowe Schoolcraft. In 1828 he contributed to the North American Review two able articles on Indian affairs, one on their government and the other containing a full review of the relations between the Indians and the British and American governments, and ascribing the then recent Indian disturbances to British instigation.

While he held the portfolio of the Department of War, he projected and advocated the formation of the American Historical Society, the objects of which institution are declared in the second article of its constitution to be "to discover, procure and preserve whatever may relate to the natural, civil, literary and ecclesiastical history of America in general, and of the United States in particular." This Society was organized on the 12th of October, 1835, the 343d anniversary of the discovery of America, and Mr. Cass was chosen its first President. He delivered before it the first annual address in the following January, a production marked with careful and erudite research, and in an easy, graceful style, which showed the natural genius of its author's mind.

During his sojourn in France, as American Minister, he published "An Historical and Statistical Account of the Island of Candia, or ancient Crete," and shortly afterwards appeared his "France; its King, Court and Government, and Three Hours at St. Cloud," in which he gives his impressions of the country in which he was for six years a resident, and a very friendly and favorable account of the character of Louis Philippe, with whom he was on terms of intimacy. Mr. Cass was also the author of many addresses before literary societies 'and other valuable papers; but I will not trespass longer upon your time, the duty of following the course of his career as a soldier, a statesman, and a man of letters has happily devolved upon our accomplished historiographer, and I will, therefore, leave to him the further development of our late fellow-member's literary life.

The resolutions were adopted, and a Committe was on motion appointed to consult with Mr. Welsh, the Historiographer, in reference to his delivering before the Society an address upon the "Life of General Cass." Mr. Hart and Dr. La Roche were appointed the Committee.

The following resolution was adopted:

Resolved, That the thanks of the Society be tendered to Hon. Wm. A. Whitehead for his considerate and acceptable gift, and that the Treasurer be directed to preserve the amount, until, by further donation or otherwise a sum sufficient be accumulated, to be securely invested, and to be known as the Binding Fund.

Hon. I. A. Lapham, of Milwaukie, Wis., sent a rubbing of a gold coin, requesting information respecting it. On motion, the communication was referred to the Committee on Numismatics, to report at our next meeting.

Mr. Price, to whom was referred the Diary of John Pemberton, made a very interesting report respecting it. On motion, his paper was referred to the Publication Committee, for publication.

An extract from a daily newspaper was read, announcing the discovery of a new Bilingual stone.

AN IMPORTANT DISCOVERY.

The Pall Mall Gazette has the following announcement:— "A discovery, of at least as vital importance for Egyptology as the celebrated Rosetta stone itself, was made about three weeks ago by a party of four German explorers—Reinisch, Rosler, Lepsius and Weidenbach—at a place called Sane, the whilom Tanis, the principal scene of Rameses II.'s enormous architectural undertakings. A stone with Greek characters upon it was found protruding from the ground, and when fully excavated proved to contain a bilingual inscription in no less than thirty-seven lines of hieroglyphics and seventy-six lines of Greek, in the most perfect state of preservation, and dating from the time of the third Ptolemy, Euergetes I. in 238 B. C. The stone measures two metres twenty-two centimetres in length, and seventy-eight centimetres in width, and is completely covered by the inscriptions. Their first attempts at editing this important inscription having failed, the travellers returned to the spot, and during a stay of two days, the 22d and 23d of April, copied the inscription most carefully, and photographed it three times. The next post will bring particulars as to the contents, and copies of the document itself."

A bill in favor of Corresponding Secretary for $2 65 was presented and ordered to be paid.

The photograph of the late Dr. Collet, presented this evening, was, on motion, directed to be framed.

The following gentlemen having been duly proposed, were unanimously elected Resident Members of the Society: •F. F. Milne, Wm. Struthers, Matthew W. Perkins, Wm. M. Swain, Henry C. Carey, Jas. H. Castle, E. E. Law, John S. Littell, Wm. H. Nevil, Charles Macalester and Wm. H. Ireland.

The following gentlemen were elected Corresponding Members: Joel Munsell, Thomas Ewbank, Henry B. Dawson, Henry R. Stiles, M.D., Solomon Alofsen and Ashbel Woodward.

The rough minutes of the meeting were read and the Society adjourned.

A. B. TAYLOR,
Secretary.

PHILADELPHIA, *August* 2, 1866.

Pursuant to notice, Messrs. Mickley and A. B. Taylor met at the room of the Society, and, there being no quorum present, adjourned.

A. B. TAYLOR,
Secretary.

PHILADELPHIA, *September* 6, 1866.

A stated meeting was held this evening, at the room of the Society. The following members were present: Messrs. Mickley, Vaux, Duane, Hart, La Roche, Phillips, Dayton, S. L. Taylor and A. B. Taylor.

The minutes of the last meeting were read and adopted.

The Committee on Numismatics reported progress, in regard to the rubbing of a gold coin which had been referred to them for examination.

The following donations were made to the Society:

From Joel Munsell, Albany, Essaie d'un Dictionaire, contenant la connoisance du monde, des sciences universelles et particulairment celle des Medailles, &c. &c., 4to, plates, A. D. 1700; Webster's Calendar; or, The Albany Almanac, for 1866, 8vo.

From Hon. Thos. Ewbank, Aboriginal Ingenuity, The Tepiti, and 4 Nos. American Artizan.

From the Mass. Historical Society, the Catalogue of its Library, 2 vols. 8vo, Boston.

From Dr. E. B. O'Callaghan, Albany, two copper coins.

From the American Philosophical Society, Proceedings of the Society. Part i., vol. x.

From Dr. La Roche, Pamphlets, &c., as follows: Academic Fallacies, by Henry Coppee, 1859; Oration on President Lincoln, by W. Binney, Providence, 1865; The Old Guard, Vol. I., New York, 1863; Discourse, by P. S. Duponceau, Philada., 1834; La France, Rome et l'Italie, Paris, 1861; Memoirs, &c., 1858.

From J. K. Curtis, New York, five volumes, viz.: Das neue ei'ofnete munzcabinet, by Joachim, Nurnberg, 1761, with plates, 1 vol. small quarto; Samlung Werkwurdiger Medaillen, for 1737, '38, '39, '40, '41, '42, '43 and '44—8 volumes in 4, by various authors, published by Johann Hieronymus Lochner, Nurnberg, v. y.

From F. Gutekunst, large photograph picture of Gen. Grant, framed.

The following letters were received and read: from I. Norris, Jr., M.D., Wm. H. Nevill, Joel Munsell, Thos. Ewbank, Henry B. Dawson, Dr. Ashbel Woodward, Dr. Henry R. Stiles and Prof. Jos. Henry, acknowledging election.

Photographs were received from Hon. I. A. Lapham, Wm. H. Nevill, Joel Munsell, Thos. Ewbank and Dr. Ashbel Woodward.

Mr. Charles H. Hart read the following interesting letter from William M. Swain, Esq., relating to some of the early telegraph men in this country.

No. 1426 North Broad Street, ⎫
PHILADELPHIA, *November* 1, 1865. ⎰

To SAMUEL HART, ESQ.

DEAR SIR: While regretting the delay which has occurred in complying with your request to furnish you (for the use of your son, who is a collector of autographs), with those of Professor Samuel F. B. Morse, the inventor of the Magnetic Telegraph, and of Hon. Amos Kendall, Postmaster-General of the United States under the administration of Gen. Andrew Jackson, during his Presidency forming one of the members of his Cabinet, and really his "right hand man." I have now the pleasure to, enclose to you the signatures of Professor Morse, Mr. Kendall, and of, several other gentlemen, some of whom if not at present highly distinguished in the world may very probably, I think, at some future time, become such as in connection with telegraphing and other sciences, professions and business.

I was called to attend a meeting of the Directors of the American Telegraph Company, held at New York on Tuesday of last week, from which I returned not until night before last, although the meeting adjourned the evening of the day of its assemblage. At it and on the subsequent day I obtained the autographs of Professor Morse and some other gentlemen prominently connected with the telegraphic enterprises of the day. These are E. S. Sanford, President American Telegraph Company; Cambridge Livingston, Esq., Counsel and Secretary; Col. Marshall Lefferts, Engineer and General Superintendent, and of Wilson G. Hunt, Esq., an eminent New York merchant, and one of the Directors of the Company. I should have obtained the autograph of Cyrus W. Field, Esq., the celebrated cable laying expeditionist, who is now one of our Directors, and who was present, but slipped out before the adjournment, and I did not see him afterwards. Mr. Kendall was too unwell to attend the meeting, but arrived in New York a day or two after. I asked him for his autograph, stated the object, and for whom it was intended. He replied, that he would furnish it to Mr. Hart's son with pleasure, but that he just then felt too nervous to write it. J. H. Wade, Esq., whose signature I send you is President of the Great Western Union Telegraph Company, and Anson Stager is General Superintendent of said Company. Both have been intimately connected with the telegraph business for many years past, if not from its commencement. The latter you may recollect as having been called to Washington by the War Department at the commencement of the rebellion, to take charge of military telegraph lines, and was commissioned as a colonel. Gustavus Swan is in charge of the telegraph office at Astor House, for the different lines extending to all parts of the country, has been identified with telegraphing from an early period. Benjamin H. Day, whose signature I send you, was the originator of the first cheap, cash daily newspaper published in this country, The New York Sun. He is a printer. His mother was a sister of the Rev. Dr. Ely, whom you may recollect as quite a celebrated preacher in this city years agone. As time rolls around, his name will become more widely and generally known and celebrated in connection with the great change from the *old fogy* system of subscription papers, when editors and publishers of newspapers acted upon the principle of having a life lease in a responsible man's name, when they got hold of it, to the *cash*, whereby a customer can obtain his newspaper as he does his hats, boots, clothing, or any other article or commodity of whatever manufacturer or seller may suit his taste or convenience. Mr. John G. Lightbody is the principal manufacturer of printing ink in this country, and especially of newspaper ink, has been for many years past, especially since the deaths of Prout, Mather and Durand. I think he is quite likely to continue such should he live for years to come. I cannot find Sanford's autograph to send it, although I obtained it. I will hereafter enclose to you Mr. Kendall's, Mr. Field's, Mr. Sanford's, Mr. O'Reilly's and some others, if I have to cut them from my filed business letters.

With very high regards, yours, &c.,

WM. M. SWAIN.

P. S.—You will observe that I have to make use of an amanuensis to do my writing for me: penmanship does not agree with the condition of my right hand now-a-days. My youngest son has in this instance been made available.

The Corresponding Secretary was, on motion, directed to procure a suitable book in which all letters written by him, pertaining to the business of the Society shall be entered, and it was further directed that this book shall be kept in the room of the Society.

A bill for postage for $1 77, in favor of the Corresponding Secretary, was presented and ordered to be paid.

A bill in favor of Mr. William S. Vaux was presented and ordered to be paid.

A bill in favor of Recording Secretary for $1 75, for 500 notices of meeting, was presented and ordered to be paid.

On motion, Dr. La Roche was authorized to procure for the Society a Photograph Album, to contain 200 pictures.

Propositions for membership, Nos. 137, 138, 139, 140, 145 and 146 were read.

The rough minutes of the meeting were read and the Society adjourned.

A. B. TAYLOR,
Secretary.

48

PHILADELPHIA, *October* 4, 1866.

A stated meeting was held this evening, at the room of the Society. The following members were present: Messrs. Mickley, Duane, Phillips, J. S. Jenks, Davis, W. T. Taylor and A. B. Taylor.

The minutes of the last meeting were read and adopted.

Dr. La Roche reported through Mr. Phillips, that he had procured a Photograph Album in accordance with the request of the Society, and presented it together with a bill for the same, amounting to $21, which was ordered to be paid.

The following report was read:

The Committee to which was referred the consideration of the best means of increasing the usefulness and securing the prosperity of the Society, reports:

That in order to fully comprehend the aims and objects of the Society, a short retrospect into its past action will be sufficient. Organized as a Numismatic Society, it was found after several years experience, that its ends were not of sufficient interest to the community to secure a proper degree of attention, and accordingly the subject of Archæology was added. Our roll of members increased considerably, and the interest taken in our proceedings was materially strengthened.

The questions now arise, How shall we continue to add to our list of members, and how rivet their attention, and secure their co-operation in the objects of our Society? When we behold the vast fields of unexplored antiquities which open on every side to our view, we wonder and are amazed. It should be borne in mind that we are not confined to any period of the existence of the world, nor to any spot within its boundaries.

"No pent-up Utica contracts our powers,
But the whole boundless Continent is ours."

In England are the Druidical remains. In Egypt, the Pyramids and the rock sculptures. In Italy are the remains of Etruscan pottery. Upon our own continent are the stone implements of the aborigines; while in Mexico and Central America there are hieroglyphic remains rivalling in interest those of ancient Thebes.

The importance of preserving everything which may remove a doubt or solve a mystery no longer remains open to discussion. Very much depends upon the labors of our own and of other similarly constituted Societies. We have a double duty to perform; we should not only collect and preserve the memorials and relics of the past, but should with diligence secure for the benefit of posterity the fleeting treasures of the present. Year after year the shores of time are washed away into the ocean of Eternity; and in the whirpool of infinity, minds and facts alike disappear. To preserve the lessons of the present while fresh in mind is a duty now easy of performance, but one which, if neglected, soon becomes impossible.

The study of Genealogy is a great assistance to antiquarian researches, but in these Middle States it has been much neglected. Our brethren of New England have been much wiser; almost every family, however insignificant, has either prepared or published its records or its pedigree, and the benefits thus conferred upon the future historian are incalculable.

We embrace among our members many varieties of the true antiquary. We have the Numismatist, the Genealogist, the Heraldic researcher, the Philologist, the Geologist, the Autographist, the Bibliographist, the Timbreophile, and the general Archæologist. It would be an easy matter for all or each of these to aid in the progress of the Society. There is no one but possesses something of interest to display. How many of our members have special knowledge of matters upon which the Society would be glad to be informed.

Our undertaking is a new one in this country, and will require the efforts of all of our members to be crowned with success. The field has long been void of an Association like our own, and we wish to impress upon our members how extremely important their individual action has become. We are at the acme of our fate, the crisis of our fortune. Two pathways stretch open before us, the one a continuation of the narrow path we have heretofore traveled, growing less and darker as we advance, and leading to obscurity; the other a grand broad avenue lighted up by fond hopes and aspirations, and leading us through most delightful grounds to fame and honor. Can we hesitate which of the two to choose? Let every member who has an object of interest, exhibit it, at a meeting of the Society. Let every member who can impart any information to the Society be sure to do so. Let every member who has a question to propose, or a doubtful point to clear up, relative to matters within our scope, at once present it to the Society, and thus invite discussion upon the subject.

As intimately connected with our prosperity and advancement, the Committee would respectfully call the attention of the Society to an evil of great magnitude, now existing amongst us, which we hope needs but to be indicated to be remedied. We regret to say that the various Standing Committees of the Society are not as active as they should be in attending to their respective duties, and in supplying the Society with matters worthy of its consideration. The Committees should remember that by this neglect of duty, the aims of our organization are either entirely abandoned, or the burthen of their performance devolves upon the shoulders of a few willing individuals, a state of things most undesirable, and one not likely to be of long continuance. Nearly a year has elapsed since the appointment of these various committees, during all which time, we are sorry to be compelled to say, they have never once assembled, nor made the slightest effort towards organization or usefulness, a condition of apathy entirely unworthy of our Society, and which, unless remedied, must eventually imperil our progress in archæological science.

In conclusion, the Committee would propose the following amendments to the By-laws, viz.: We propose striking out Chapter V. of the By-laws, and inserting in place thereof the following:

CHAPTER V.

Of Standing Committees and their Duties.

ART. I. The Standing Committees of the Society shall each be composed of three Resident Members, who shall be elected annually, at the stated meeting in December, and shall be as follows:

I. On Numismatics, of which the Curator of Numismatics shall be a member "ex-officio." The duties of this Committee shall be to collect and preserve matters relative to the science of Numismatics, and to present to the Society such questions as it may think proper, and to prepare replies to such inquiries as may from time to time be referred to it.

II. On Antiquities, of which the Curator of Antiquities shall be a member "ex-officio." The duties of this Committee shall be to collect and preserve matters relative to archæological research, and to present to the Society such questions as it may think proper, and to prepare replies to such inquiries as may from time to time be referred to it.

III. On Genealogy, of which the Historiographer shall be a member "ex-officio." The duties of this Committee shall be to collect and preserve all matter germane to the science of Genealogy, and to present to the Society such questions as it may think proper, and to prepare replies to such inquiries as may from time to time be referred to it.

IV. On Library, of which the Librarian shall be a member "ex-officio." The duties of this Committee shall be to procure, with the funds placed at its disposal by the Society, such works as may be directed to be purchased, and to report from time to time what books it may consider most desirable to be obtained for the Society. It shall also be its duty to collect all such books, papers, pamphlets, &c., as it may deem proper to be placed in the library. The Committee shall have power to make such exchanges of duplicates as may to it appear desirable.

V. On Hall. The Hall Committee shall have the general care of the Hall; and shall provide such conveniences as may be necessary for the accommodation of the officers and members of the Society. It shall be the duty of this Committee to have the room opened in proper time for all stated or special meetings of the Society, or at other times when so directed by the Society.

VI. On Publication, of which the Recording Secretary shall be a member "ex-officio." The duty of this Committee shall be to take charge of the publication of the proceedings of this Society, or such other publications as the Society may from time to time direct.

VII. On Finance, of which the Treasurer shall be a member "ex-officio." The duties of this Committee shall be to supervise the operations of the Treasury, and to examine and certify to the correctness of all bills, which shall be signed by at least two members of the Committee, previous to being paid by the Treasurer.

We propose striking out in Article V., Chapter I. of the By-laws, the words "except on an order from the President, countersigned by the Recording Secretary," and inserting in their place the following, "unless by direction of the Finance Committee."

WILLIAM DUANE,
HENRY PHILLIPS, JR., } *Committee.*
A. B. TAYLOR,

The following donations were made to the Society:

From Mr. Brock, of Richmond, Va., the tracing of a medal, together with the following description of it: The enclosed tracing is from a silver medal which was in the possession of the Virginia Historical Society before the war, but as the library and collections of the Society were stored in the Mechanic's Institute (the buildings used by the Confederate War Department), they were destroyed by fire in April, 1865. No *original* now exists. The medal was supposed to be one of a number given by the early settlers of Virginia to the chiefs of the several Indian tribes. It was an engraved medal, and not struck.

From Mr. Price, Friend's Miscellany, 12 vols., accompanied by a letter.

The following communication from Mr. Charles H. Hart, in reference to the decease of Dr. Hawks, was presented by Mr. Phillips.

Since our last meeting our ranks have been again invaded by the hand of death, which has removed from our fellowship the Rev. Dr. Hawks, a Corresponding Member of this Society. Dr. Hawks died at New York on the 27th of last month, in the sixty-ninth year of his age. He was a native of North Carolina, and at the time of his decease, was engaged upon a history of his mother State, the first volume of which was published nearly ten years since. He was educated for the Bar, and practiced his profession for about six years, when believing he was better fitted for the ministry, he was ordained a Minister of the Protestant Episcopal Church, by Bishop Ravenscroft of North Carolina, and soon after became an assistant to the venerable Bishop White, at St. James' Church, in this city.

He was a man of the most brilliant eloquence and profound scholarship, and his loss will be deeply felt not only in the denomination to which he belonged, but to society and letters as well. In concluding, I beg leave to offer the following resolutions for the consideration of the Society.

Resolved, That this Society has heard with emotions of profound sorrow and deep regret of the decease of its late fellow correspondent, the Rev. Francis Lister Hawks, DD., L.L.D., and that by this sudden and sad event the Society has been deprived of one of its most brilliant ornaments; the church of one of its truest teachers and ablest expounders, and the community of letters, of one of its noblest compeers.

Resolved, That a copy of these resolutions be entered upon our minutes, as a memorial of our appreciation of his worth and as a tribute of respect to his memory, and that the Historiographer be requested to prepare the customary memoir.

The resolutions proposed were adopted.

A very interesting paper, by Mr. Phillips, on "The Pleasures of Numismatic Science," was read by its author, and referred for publication.

The following entertaining letter was read by Mr. Duane, from Adjutant-General Daniel Parker to Mr. Duane's grandfather, Col. William Duane, Adjutant-General U. S. A.

FREDERICKTOWN, *Aug.* 27, 1814.

DEAR SIR: In addition to the many laughable stories which you will hear of the late movements at Washington and its vicinity, allow me to tell you that after packing our public papers, &c., and while I was at dinner on Monday, Gen. Armstrong sent to me to join him on horseback in one hour. I went to the President's, where the Cabinet was in conclave, and I was for half an hour talking with the Queen. At about 6 P.M. the President, Gen. Armstrong, Mr. Jones, Mr. Rush, a Mr. Carrol (who knows the country, &c.) and myself set out, not till Mrs. M. had given me a particular charge to take care of her husband, (seeing I was the youngest and most active,) and must stick to him and bring him back. This I promised without reserve, as I very well knew we should keep out of danger. We went about 12 miles, to the camp of Gen. Winder, on the road to Marlboro, where we slept on the floor, using our saddles for pillows. We spent the next morning helping Gen. W. *do nothing*, for he never reconnoitered the enemy's camp, altho' he had more than 400 dragoons. Our militia were kept in the hot sun, and we remained on the ground like militia generals until 2 o'clock, when we returned half way to Washington, dined, and then repaired to the President's House. I reported to Mrs. M., went to see some ladies whose husbands were absent, &c. At 11 o'clock General A. desired me to be ready in the morning. The General, Mr. Campbell and lady took breakfast with me, and then I attended the two ministers to Gen. W.'s headquarters near the Capitol.

We found the President, Mr. Jones and Mr. Rush. Col. Monroe had been gone some time, we were told, to the army near Bladensburg; in short he was the Berthier of the day, as I found when we joined, for he had formed the troops and disposed the line of Battle, with what skill I must inform you at another time. Our regular troops never fired a musket. The President waited to see the first rockets let off by the enemy, and then left the field, leaving Genl. W., Generalissimo. Genl. A. believed he had a right to see the fight and staid behind. I had carried an order to bring a Regt. of militia, and did not

5

join them on the field till the firing had commenced on both
sides, tho' I had reported to Genl. W. the situation of the
Regt. to which I had been sent, and had offered my further
services, while he was doing the duty of a battalion officer,
cheering the light troops on his left without a single man of
his staff near him, tho' his aids were very numerous before the
firing commenced. When the line broke the whole began to
run and the Genl. ordered a retreat. I then joined Genl. A.
with Winder and carried a message or two to make the
militia run faster, *and form in Washington.* After this I
kept with the minister, and knowing the route across the fields
we made a direct line to the Capitol. The column of our troops
came up at the time we arrived. Gen. W. had taken his measures to retreat to Georgetown. He spoke with Genl. A. and
with Col. Monroe, and we parted. The Colonel went over the
Potomac to the Ancient Dominion, where the President had
gone as well as Jones and others. Campbell was taking care
of his wife on his way to this place, the Cabinet rendezvous.
Genl. A. and myself slept that night near Montgomery C. H.
with an acquaintance of mine, and the next day saw Gen. W.
and his veterans at the C. H.

The war office papers were sent here. The State papers
were sent to Va. The treasury papers here, and the Navy on
the road. We arrived yesterday, have taken rooms, and are
now attending to the business of the War Dept. with our guard
sufficient to give one centinel at the door. The other depart-
ments are not yet in operation: the War Dept. is as regular
as it was at Washington.

You cannot fancy such ridiculous scenes as I have witnessed
this week. Cockburn entered the city with only 100 men and
commenced his burning about 9 o'clock. The enemy encamped
previously near Gallatin's house. It is impossible to get any
correct information yet from Washington.

Yours,

PARKER.

P. S.—You will see that this is not a public document, and
I should be ashamed to hear of any part of the story as coming
from me.

Hon. Fred. W. Seward, of Washington, having been duly
proposed, was unanimously elected an Honorary Member of
the Society.

Messrs. L. Montgomery Bond, Theodore Frothingham and
Edward S. Clarke, having been duly proposed, were unanimously elected Resident Members of the Society.

Dr. N. B. Shurtleff, of Boston, was unanimously elected a Corresponding Member of the Society.

Proposition No. 147 was read.

The rough minutes of the meeting were read and the Society adjourned.

A. B. TAYLOR,
Secretary.

PHILADELPHIA, *November* 1, 1866.

A stated meeting was held this evening, at the room of the Society. The following members were present: Messrs. Mickley, Vaux, Duane, Chandler, Welsh, Phillips, Hart, Farnum, Dayton, W. J. Jenks, W. T. Taylor and A. B. Taylor.

The minutes of the last meeting were read and adopted.

The following donations were made to the Society.

From Mr. Duane, Wood's Prospect of New England, 1 vol. sm. 4to, and a picture of the old Masonic Hall.

On motion of Mr. Chandler, the Hall Committee were directed to have this picture framed.

From Hon. R. C. Winthrop, Proceedings of the Massachusetts Historical Society for 1864, '65.

From Mr. Hart, a Scrap-Book, and a Pamphlet, entitled A Letter on Paper Money, by Erick Bollman, M.D.

From Mr. Phillips, The Rhode Island Colonial Records, 7 vols. 8vo; also, Military Laws, &c., published in Washington, 1813, 1 vol. 12mo, and an 8vo. vol. of Catalogues.

From Mr. Horace H. Furness, a gold coin of the French Revolution, 1851, ten francs value, accompanied by a letter.

Mr. Charles H. Hart, then made the following announcement:

We are called upon this evening to record the decease of another of our members, Dr. Robert W. Gibbes, Honorary Vice-President for the State of South Carolina. Dr. Gibbes died at the residence of his son, in the city of New York, on the 15th of last month. He was born in Charleston, S. C., July 8th, 1809, and was consequently in his fifty-eighth year, was graduated at the University of South Carolina, and re-

ceived the degree of M. D. in 1830, when he removed to
Columbia, of which city he was twice Mayor, and commenced
the practice of his profession. His contributions to science
are many, and varied, perhaps the most important of which
were his "Memoir of the Fossil Genus Basilosaurus," and
"Monograph of the Fossil Squalidæ of the United States,"
and not the least interesting his lecture on "The Present
Earth, the Remains of a Former World." He also contributed
many valuable articles to the "Southern Quarterly Review,"
"The American Journal of Medical Science," and the publications of the Smithsonian Institution and the Academy of
Natural Sciences, in this city. In 1853 he commenced publishing his "Documentary History of South Carolina," which
extended to three volumes, and was a work which showed
much care and judgment as an editor. Dr. Gibbes was an
ardent antiquarian and a devoted lover of the fine arts, but
unhappily his rare collection of pictures and statuary, his
library and museum, are now dust and ashes, having been
consumed with his house in the destruction of Columbia, in
1865, during the presence of Sherman's army. Throughout
the disastrous war which terminated in that year of ruin, he
served his native State as surgeon-in-chief, winning for himself
in that position the esteem and affection of friends and enemies
alike, for his skill, humanity and administrative ability. In
conclusion, I would submit the following:

WHEREAS, It has pleased the Divine Will to remove from
his earthly usefulness Robert Wilson Gibbes, M.D., of Columbia, South Carolina, one of the Honorary Vice-Presidents of
this Society, be it

Resolved, That in the death of Dr. Gibbes, this Society has
lost one of its most accomplished members and ardent antiquarians; an erudite scholar and able physician, an exemplary
citizen and enlightened gentleman, whose various volumes in
the several branches of History, Science and Antiquity fully
attest to his learning, ability and industry.

Resolved, That these resolutions be entered in full upon the
minutes of this meeting, and the customary memoir be prepared.

The resolutions were seconded and adopted.

A communication from the Editor of the Historical Magazine was read by the Corresponding Secretary.

A letter from Hon. F. W. Seward was received accepting
election, and returning thanks, also enclosing his photograph.

Photographs were received from Hon. Robert C. Winthrop,
R. Alonzo Brock and Dr. W. T. Taylor.

A letter from Essex Institute, Salem, Mass., was read.

An interesting paper on National Medals, &c., by Mr. Hart, was read by its author.

On motion, the subscription to the N. E. Historical and Genealogical Register was directed to be continued for next year.

Mr. Welsh notified the Society that at its next stated meeting he would be prepared to read a memoir on the late General Cass.

On motion, the Hall Committee was directed to purchase a Stove.

Messrs. Mickley, Dayton and Hart were appointed a Committee to examine a Fire-Proof Safe, which had been offered to the Society, with directions to purchase it, if satisfactory to the Committee.

The following resolution offered by Mr. Phillips was adopted:

Resolved, That Messrs. Lovett, Warner and Key, be requested to furnish to the Society lists of the dies severally prepared by them, together with any information they can give respecting them, as to the numbers struck, varieties of metals, &c.

The amendments to the By-laws proposed at the last meeting were adopted.

It was on motion resolved, that when we adjourn, we adjourn to meet on the third Thursday of this month, for the purpose of hearing the continuation of Mr. Hart's paper on National Medals, &c.

The Chairman appointed a Committee, consisting of Messrs. Vaux, Dayton and W. J. Jenks, to nominate officers and committees for the Society for the ensuing year.

Mr. A. S. Jenks having been duly proposed, was unanimously elected a Resident Member of the Society.

Rev. Elias Nason, of Boston, was elected a Corresponding Member of the Society.

Proposition No. 149 was read.

The rough minutes of the meeting were read and the Society adjourned.

A. B. Taylor,
Secretary.

PHILADELPHIA, *November* 15, 1866.

Pursuant to adjournment, a meeting was held this evening, at the room of the Society, the following members being present: Messrs. Vaux, Hart, Chandler, Phillips, W. T. Taylor and A. B. Taylor.

In the absence of the President, Vice-President Vaux took the chair.

The business of the meeting having been announced, Mr. Hart read the continuation of his paper on American Medals. After having been read, the paper was, on motion, referred to the Publication Committee.

There being no further business before the Society, on motion, adjourned.

A. B. TAYLOR,
Secretary.

PHILADELPHIA, *December* 6, 1866.

A stated meeting was held this evening, at the room of the Society. The following members were present: Messrs. Mickley, Vaux, Duane, Clay, Ducommun, W. J. Jenks, Hart, Phillips, La Roche, Creighton, S. L. Taylor and A. B. Taylor.

The minutes of the last meeting were read and adopted.

The following donations were made to the Society:

From Rev. Eugene Vetromile, his Indian Almanac, his Indian Prayer Book, and "The Abnakis and their History."

From Mr. Edward E. Law, the author, an 8vo. vol., entitled "Portraits of the Saviour."

From the Publishers, the November number of the American Journal of Numismatics.

From Mr. R. Alonzo Brock, a Coupon Bond for £100, of Commonwealth of Virginia, published in 185–.

From Mr. Hamilton Creighton, six copper coins.

From Mr. W. H. Key, four Medals, in copper, bronzed, as follows:

No. 1. *Obv.* A head of Liberty, with flowing hair, encircled by a fillet and stars; above, "Light, Liberty, Law." *Rev.* The

New York Free Academy was founded 1847, by Act of the Legislature and vote of the citizens; and its name was changed 1866, by Act taking effect May 1, to "College of the City of New York." Size, 38.

No. 2. *Obv.* Head of Wesley; above, "The best of all is, God is with us." *Rev.* "Jesus loves me and I must love Jesus. Blessed are they that do his commandments, that they may have right to the tree of life." . Size, 24.

No. 3. *Obv.* A boy ascending rocks, and holding a streamer, on which are the words "Never say can't." *Rev.* "Whatsoever thy hand findeth to do, do it with thy might. I can do all things through Christ, which strengtheneth me." Size, 24.

No. 4. *Obv.* A child praying. *Rev.* "Suffer little children to come unto me, and forbid them not, for of such is the kingdom of God." Size, 24.

The following letters were read: from Rev. S. K. Lothrop, of Boston, acknowledging his election, and returning thanks, also enclosing photograph; from Rev. Elias Nason, of Massachusetts, acknowledging his election, and returning thanks; from S. Alofsen, of Jersey City, acknowledging his election, and enclosing $25, with his photograph.

On motion of Mr. Hart, it was resolved, that the thanks of this Society be tendered to Solomon Alofsen, Esq., of Jersey City, for his considerate and acceptable gift, and that the Treasurer be directed to add the donation to the amount already in hand, known as the "Binding Fund."

A letter was read from Mr. Joseph Diver, declining membership.

The President reported that the gold piece from Mr. Lapham, which had been referred to him for identification, was a gold coin of Robert of Geneva, Archbishop, and Count of Cambrai, France, from 1368 to 1378.

On motion, the Corresponding Secretary was directed to send the information to Mr. Lapham.

A bill in favor of the Corresponding Secretary, for ninety-eight cents, was presented and ordered to be paid.

The Committee appointed to examine a Fire Proof Safe, reported that it had purchased the Safe for $30, and that it was in the room.

The Hall Committee reported that it had bought a stove for $8, which was also in the room.

On motion of Mr. Ducommun, the Curator of Numismatics was directed to deposit the collection in his possession in the Safe of the Society.

The Committee on Nominations reported the following list of officers and committees for the ensuing year:

President—Joseph J. Mickley.

Vice-Presidents—William P. Chandler, William S. Vaux and William Duane.

Honorary Vice-Presidents—John Marshall Brown, Esq., of Portland, Maine; Hon. J. W. Patterson, of New Hampshire; Hon. Robert C. Winthrop, of Boston, Massachusetts; Hon. Samuel G. Arnold, of Providence, Rhode Island; Hon. William A. Buckingham, of Norwich, Connecticut; J. Carson Brevoort, Esq., of Brooklyn, New York; Hon. Richard S. Field, of Princeton, New Jersey; Prof. Joseph Henry, of District of Columbia; Hon. Reverdy Johnson, of Baltimore, Maryland; Hon. Thomas J. Randolph, of Virginia, and Hon. I. A. Lapham, of Wisconsin.

Recording Secretary—Charles H. Hart.

Corresponding Secretary—A. B. Taylor.

Treasurer—Henry Phillips, Jr.

Historiographer—William H. Welsh.

Curator of Numismatics—William J. Jenks.

Curator of Antiquities—Robert C. Davis.

Librarian—W. B. Dayton.

Committee on Hall—W. T. Taylor, M.D , C. H. Hart and C. P. La Roche, M.D.

Committee on Library—W. B. Dayton, S. H. Fulton and S. L. Taylor.

Committee on Numismatics—Edward S. Clarke, Robert C. Davis and William J. Jenks.

Committee on Antiquities—Joseph A. Clay, William S. Vaux and Robert C. Davis.

Committee on Genealogy—Eli K. Price, William P. Chandler and William H. Welsh.

Committee on Publication—H. Phillips, Jr., William S. Vaux and A. B. Taylor.

Committee on Finance—William Duane, H. Ducommun and H. Phillips, Jr.

In addition to these nominations, the following nominations were made by Mr. Hart:

Vice-President—Eli K. Price.
Hon. Vice-President—Rt. Rev. Wm. Ingraham Kip, D.D., of California.
Recording Secretary—A. B. Taylor.

By Mr. Phillips:

Corresponding Secretary—Charles H. Hart.
Librarian—Samuel L. Taylor.

An election was ordered. Messrs. S. L. Taylor and William Duane were appointed tellers, who duly reported that the following officers had been elected for the next year.

President—Joseph J. Mickley.
Vice-Presidents—William P. Chandler, William S. Vaux, William Duane and Eli K. Price.
Honorary Vice-Presidents—As nominated.
Recording Secretary—A. B. Taylor.
Corresponding Secretary—Charles H. Hart.
Librarian—S. L. Taylor.

And all other officers and committees, as nominated by the Committee.

On motion, the Publication Committee was directed to have the minutes of the Society prepared for Publication.

On motion, the Treasurer was directed to renew the lease of the room for one year, from the first of January next, at the same rate as for the present year, $150.

The Corresponding Secretary was directed to have the list of officers and committees printed.

On motion of Mr. Phillips, the various officers and committees elected to-night, were requested to signify their acceptance of the positions to which they have been chosen.

Mr. William B. Trask, of Boston, having been duly proposed, was elected Corresponding Member of the Society.

Propositions Nos. 150, 151, 152 and 153 were read.

The rough minutes of the meeting were read and the Society adjourned.

A. B. TAYLOR,
Secretary.

APPENDIX.

HALL.

JAMES HALL, of Allentown, Pa., was born at Litiz, Lancaster county, Pa., on the 23d of August, 1773; at an early age he left that place and went to Bethlehem, where he lived a number of years, and for the last thirty or thirty-five years resided at Allentown. He led a private life excepting six years, in which he held the office of Register of Wills and Recorder in Lehigh county, to which office he was appointed by Governor Wolff. After his retirement from office, he devoted his time to literature and numismatics; for the latter he had a particular fondness, not only to collect coins, but more particularly to study them. Probably no other individual in this country possessed a better knowledge of the science than he did. He corresponded with some distinguished numismatists of Europe on the subject. He commenced collecting coins when he was but fifteen years of age, in 1788; his collection was not large, but very choice; in consequence of losing his sight in 1853, he sold his collection for $850, and also sold his Numismatic. Library. He was a man of sound judgment, an extraordinary memory, and of an unblemished character.

He died on the 26th of November, 1861, aged 88 years, 3 months and 3 days.   J. J. M.

COLLET.

MARK WILKS COLLET, was born in the town of Patterson, New Jersey, in the year 1826.

His father was a grandson of the Revd. James Wilks, Chaplain and Registrar to the Bishop of Sodor and Mann; his mother, the daughter of Joshua M. Wallace, Esq., of Burlington, New Jersey.

Dr. Collet's education was with the Revd. R. W. Harris, of White Plains, New York; at the age of fifteen he entered the Military Academy at West Point. After three years of good standing at this Institution, his health failing, he was obliged to resign. He was the classmate of Generals Franklin, McClellan, and Stonewall Jackson. After this he began the study of medicine in Philadelphia, and early in the year 1848, graduated at the Jefferson College. Expecting to be obliged to go abroad before his class graduated, he requested from the professors a private examination, which was granted, and he received the testimony and congratulations of each one, on his proficiency. From this time he pursued the practice of medicine, until the breaking out of the Rebellion, when feeling his own capacity, as well as the duty to serve his country, he offered himself to his native State, and received a commission as Major in the Third Regiment, New Jersey Volunteers.

History tells of the gallantry and bravery of the New Jersey Brigade, in which General Kearney took such pride; and among the leaders of these brave men, was none braver, truer, or a more accomplished officer than the subject of this memoir, soon advanced to the Coloncley of the First New Jersey Volunteers.

After leading his regiment through many of the battles on the Peninsula, and at Manassa, Antietam, and on the Rappahannock, the disastrous one of the 3d of May, 1863, closed the career of this soldier and patriot. He fell at Salem Church, near Fredericksburg, and was interred by the enemy, commanded by the rebel General Wilcox, another of his classmates at West Point. Subsequently his remains were recovered, and now rest in the churchyard of St. James the Less, near Philadelphia.　　　　　R. C.

DAVIDS.

It is a source of regret to the Society, that of its late lamented fellow member, Mr. Richard W. Davids, no better memorial could be obtained from the members of his family than the brief sketch hereto annexed. Mr. Davids was one of the most thorough antiquarians among the members of our Society, and his knowledge of mediæval coinage and general archæology, was very extensive. The wound inflicted by his loss upon the Society has not yet healed, and many poignant regrets are still felt at his untimely death in the service of his country.

Richard Wistar Davids, was born in New York, August 30, 1826, and removed to Philadelphia at an early age.

He entered the 118th Regiment, Pennsylvania Volunteers, August, 1862, and after enduring the hardships to which the Army of the Potomac was exposed, was killed at the battle of Gettysburg, July 2, 1863.   D.

VAUX.

IN the loss of its youngest member, the Society had another illustration of the fact, that the fairest flowers are earliest plucked.

Frederic Graff Vaux, was the only child of William S. and Emily G. Vaux, both members of well known families of this city, where he was born March 15, 1846. During the limited period of his connection with this Institution, he secured the respect and affectionate regard of all its members, and his kindly disposition, exemplary conduct and diligent attention to, and warm interest in the subjects which engaged the consideration of the Society, were especially noteworthy. His memory, especially for dates and names (a qualification so important in the numismatist and antiquarian), was very remarkable. Had he been spared, we doubt not his career would have been highly useful and honorable.

August 4, 1864, after a lingering illness, at the early age of eighteen, and while surrounded by every thing that could secure comfort, luxury and pleasure, he died the death of a young Christian.   W. P. C.

SOME OBSERVATIONS

ON

EARLY CURRENCY OF MARYLAND.

A PAPER READ BEFORE

" The Numismatic and Antiquarian Society of Philadelphia,"

THURSDAY EVENING, JUNE 7, 1865,

BY

HENRY PHILLIPS, Jr.

EARLY CURRENCY OF MARYLAND.

To Maryland, settled by British subjects, was brought the currency of their home. Silver and gold doubtless existed among them, although the amount could be but small, while the necessity of constant remittances to the mother country for merchandize ever in demand (and hence the impossibility of retaining a currency of specie in a state of colonial dependance) soon caused a change in the actual value of the coin: the operation of the laws of supply and demand being invariable. The inconveniences caused by the loss of their circulating medium the inhabitants sought to remedy by various expedients, and among them appear wampum and its congeners, tobacco, coinage, tobacco notes, and finally, bills of credit. Upon the nature, varieties and uses of wampum, it is not the present intention to dilate: the subject deserves a strict historical collation, which it is hoped may by us, at some future time, be performed. We therefore pass at once to the great staple, *tobacco*.

A law of Maryland, passed in 1639, five years after the first settlements therein, makes tobacco a legal tender, at the rate of five shillings sterling for every thirty pounds of the staple, being at the rate of twopence per pound. To this result Virginia had led the way: in that province in 1618, tobacco had been declared a legal tender at three shillings per pound, soon, however, falling to a more moderate value. This was the standard at which, in 1620, wives were sold to the Virginia planters, at prices ranging from one hundred to one hundred and fifty pounds of tobacco at threepence per pound. In 1645, the General Council of the Province resolved to issue a copper coinage for circulation of the value of 2d., 3d., 6d. and 9d., on which were to be impressed two rings, one to contain the date, and the other a suitable motto. These pieces, if they were ever actually coined, have not reached the present time.*

In 1661, the Assembly of Maryland, "by reason of the great hindrance to the Colony in trade for want of money," erected a mint, and provided for the coinage of silver money, of sterling alloy, at the rate of ninepence sterling for every shilling currency, and the smaller pieces in the same proportion. This action, it will be observed, makes a difference of twenty-five per cent. between the sterling and the currency value of the shilling, and raises the dollar to five shillings sevenpence halfpenny.

Folkes† speaks of these coins as being shillings, half shillings, and groats; of handsome execution, but lacking above twopence in the shilling of the sterling value. In order to send these coins into circulation, it was enacted, in the following year, that every householder in the province should be obliged to take of them ten shillings per poll for every inhabitant within his dwelling, and to make payment therefor in tobacco, at twopence per pound. This law was confirmed and continued in 1676, but over the fate and termination of this coinage a mystery seems to hang: ten years later, when, by statute, the value of the coin then current in the Colony, was regulated, no mention whatever is made of these coins. New England shillings and sixpences were rated at their nominal value, though they were really only worth eightpence and fourpence. French crowns, pieces of eight and rix dollars were to pass for six shillings; ducatoons at seven shillings and sixpence; Spanish milled dollars previously rated at four shillings and sixpence, then at five shillings seven and a halfpence, were now to pass current for six shillings. All other foreign silver and gold coins were to be estimated at threepence in the shilling over their value.

An act passed in 1704, which regulated the interest to be

---

* Streeter's paper on the Maryland Currency. Dickeson gives these pieces to Virginia.

† Edition, 1763, p. 98.

permitted on loans, prescribes an interest of six per cent. on money contracts, but allows eight per cent. on those wherein tobacco should enter. In the same year *hemp* and *flax* were declared to be a legal tender for the payment of one-fourth of any debt: the former being estimated at sixpence, and the latter at fourpence per pound.

For forging or clipping the coin made current in the Province, the Act of 1707 inflicts the following punishments: on a first conviction, whipping, cropping of the ears and pillorying; on the second offence, branding and banishment. Such remained the law of the land until 1729, when, in consequence of silver being cut into small pieces, halves, quarters, eighths and six-teenths, to supply the then greatly felt want of small change, and being therefore received only by weight, the sanitary provisions of this act were no longer needful for the security of the Province, and it was therefore repealed.

The proclamation issued in the sixth year of Queen Anne, for establishing the rates of foreign coins in the American plantations, met in its workings with some difficulties, to obviate which, Parliament, in 1707, enacted it into a law, and the Assembly of Maryland in the following year did the same. The following table shows the rates thereby established:

Name.	Weight.		Intrinsic Value.		Current Value.		
	dwt.	*gr.*	*s.*	*d.*	*s.*	*d.*	*qr.*
Sevill piece of eight, old plate, .	17	12	4	6	6	0	0
Sevill piece of eight, new plate, .	14	0	3	7½	4	9	2⅔
Mexico piece of eight, ...	17	12	4	6	6	0	0
Pillar piece of eight, ...	17	12	4	6¾	6	0	0
Peru piece of eight, old plate, . .	17	12	4	5¾	5	10	2⅔
Cross Dollars, ...	18	4	4	4½	5	10	2⅔
Ducatoon of Flanders, ...	20	21	5	6	7	4	0
Ficu of France, or silver Lewis, .	17	12	4	6	6	0	0
3 gilders pieces of Holland, . .	20	7	5	2¼	6	11	3⅞
Crusadoes of Portugal, ...	11	4	2	10¼	3	9	2¼
Old Rix Dollar of the Empire, . .	18	10	4	6	6	0	0

The Act speaks of *Dog Dollars* as being the money which was most plentiful in the Province, and with which the inhabitants were best acquainted: upon them the value of four shillings

6

and sixpence was placed. In the laws of Pennsylvania, these coins are frequently mentioned as the Lion or Dog Dollars, and are there rated in 1723 at five shillings.

In 1713, the Maryland Assembly regulated the manner in which tobacco, as a legal tender, was to be offered and received in payment of debts, but the Act neglects to mention the rate at which it is to be valued. This, however, we find from a subsequent Act of the same session, was about one penny per pound, or fifty shillings currency, equal to six hundred pounds of tobacco: twenty pounds sterling money were valued at five thousand pounds of the staple. At this rate it permanently remained, being in 1732, made a legal tender at that rate.

To encourage still more the importation of gold and silver, of which the want was greatly felt by the inhabitants, an Act of Assembly, passed in 1729, gives an additional premium of fifteen per cent. upon all such monies paid in as duties over and above the advanced rates established in 1708. The person who should claim the benefit of this law, was obliged to make oath that the money had not been previously exported from the Province, so that on its return it might be entitled to this allowance. This premium would make a rise in the value of the dollar to about forty-eight per cent., or about seven shillings in currency. A table adopted in 1763, as a standard for tobacco payments, reads as follows:

Johannes, to be worth	920 pounds of tobacco.
Half Johannes,	460 " "
Moidore,	348 " "
English Guinea,	272 " "
French Guinea,	268 " "
Spanish pistoles, not lighter than 4 dwt. 6 gr.,	216 " "
French milled pistoles,	212 " "
Arabian chequins,	108 " "
Other gold coin (German excepted), by the dwt.,	50 " "
French Silver Crowns,	60 " "
Spanish milled pieces of eight,	60 " "
Other good coined Spanish silver, per oz.,	68 " "

In 1773, we find the first and apparently entirely unexpected mention made of the dollar being valued at *seven shillings* and

sixpence, the rate at which it finally settled. In this year,
(ch. xxx.,) we find an Act valuing tobacco at one shilling and
sixpence for twelve pounds, which, being properly carried out,
will make the value of the dollar the amount above stated.
An Act passed this session (ch. xxxiii.), for the discharge of
the public debts, provides for their payment at the valuation of
$1⅔ in bills of credit for every one hundred pounds of tobacco,
and the dollar to be equal to seven shillings and sixpence. The
exact time when, and the reason why this change took place,
cannot with certainty be ascertained: only this *result* is known.

Such were the fluctuations of the dollar—established in
1686 at four shillings and sixpence, in 1708 at six shillings,
and in 1773, appearing as seven shillings and sixpence. This
latter valuation is followed by the Act of 1781, after the independence of the State, which affixed rates to foreign coins
thereafter to be current. The following was the table adopted:

			£	s.	d.
Johannes, weighing	18 dwt.,	. . .	6	0	0
Half Johannes,	9 dwt.,	. .	3	0	0
Moidores,	6 dwt. 18 gr.,	. . .	2	5	0
English Guineas,	5 dwt. 6 gr.,	. .	1	15	0
French Guineas,	5 dwt. 5 gr.,	. . .	1	14	6
Doubloons,	17 dwt.,	. . .	5	12	0
Spanish pistoles,	4 dwt. 6 gr.,	. . .	1	8	0
French milled pistoles,	4 dwt. 4 gr.,	.	1	7	6
Arabian chequins,	2 dwt. 3 gr.,	. .	0	13	9
Other gold coin (German excepted), by the dwt.,		. .	0	6	8
English milled Crowns,	. . .	.	0	8	4
Other milled silver,	. . . .	.	0	8	4
French silver Crowns,	. .	.	0	8	4
Spanish milled pieces of eight, .	. . .		0	7	6
Other good coined Spanish silver, per oz., .	. .	.	0	8	6
Any other gold coin of the same fineness, of Portugal or Spain,					
per oz., ...		.	6	13	4

A currency of paper founded upon tobacco, called *Inspection
Notes*, arose in 1763, and we are told that as late as the beginning of the present century it still existed to a limited extent.
The system was akin to and based upon that which had existed
for some years previous in Virginia, where it bore the name,

yet more expressive, of tobacco notes. The staple was placed by the producer or owner in the public warehouses for his county, was duly inspected and branded by the proper officer, who gave for it a receipt, specifying the quality and quantity of the deposit: this receipt, or as it was called, Inspection Note, was a *legal tender* for all purposes in the county wherein it was issued, and the holders possessed the right of obtaining at any time from the storehouses the amount, &c., of tobacco, which the face of the note called for. This currency superseded that of the staple, which was then declared no longer to be a legal tender.

The history of the Bills of Credit issued by Maryland we hope to be able to lay before the Society at some future time.

A PAPER READ BEFORE

The Numismatic and Antiquarian Society

OF PHILADELPHIA,

On Thursday Evening, October 5, 1865.

BY

ALFRED B. TAYLOR.

PHILADELPHIA:
1867.

GOLDEN RELICS FROM CHIRIQUI.

THE curious and interesting relics which I have the pleasure of exhibiting this evening, are part of a large lot that was found in 1859, in one of the numerous huacas or burying grounds in the province of Chiriqui,* (New Granada), about 180 miles southwest of the city of Panama.

There are nine specimens, varying in length from $1\frac{3}{16}$ inches to 3 inches, and weighing from 130 to 1338 grains; they vary considerably in color, some of them being bright yellow, while others are apparently alloyed more or less with copper.

No. 1. A human figure with the head of a monster; the mouth open, and horns projecting from the end of the nostrils, the head surmounted by a sort of crown, projections from which on either side, form an ornamental framework around the whole figure. Size, 2 inches wide, $1\frac{7}{8}$ inches high. Weight, 1 oz. 4 dwt. 14 grs.

No. 2. The representation of an animal not described in the books; large globular projecting eyes; mouth open; the legs spread out horizontally, flattened into plates, each one terminating in a dolphin's head; two tails, each terminating in an arrowhead. Size, $2\frac{7}{8}$ inches wide, 3 inches long. Weight, 2 oz. $6\frac{1}{2}$ dwts.

No. 3. A frog, with large protruding eyes, the fore-legs terminating in rings. Size, $\frac{3}{4}$ inches wide, $1\frac{1}{8}$ inches long. Weight, 5 dwt. 10 grs.

No. 4. An obscene human figure, with the head of a monster, and a tail pointed at the end, extending over the head in the form of a hoop, and held by both hands. Size, $1\frac{1}{8}$ inches wide, $1\frac{5}{16}$ inches high. Weight, 6 dwt. 4 grs.

* David, the capitol of Chiriqui, is in about 8° 17′ N., by 82° 30′ W.

No. 5. The head of an alligator, evidently designed for a bell, being hollow, and having inside a ball of gold ¾ inch in diameter; the mouth open, and the lower and upper jaw each furnished with eight long teeth, so arranged as to prevent the ball from falling out. The eyes are oval, large and prominent; upon the extremity of the nostrils is a large projection; under the lower jaw is a ring, not soldered on, but made in the original casting, which is the case with each one of these nine pieces, some of them having two rings, while others have only one. Size, $1\frac{5}{16}$ inch wide, 2 inches long, $1\frac{1}{4}$ inches high. Weight, 2 oz. 15 dwt. 18 grs.

No. 6. An alligator, the tail bent up and resting upon the back; the forelegs terminating in rings. Size, ⅝ inch wide, 2 inches long. Weight, 6 dwt. 6 grs.

No. 7. An obscene human figure, with the head of a monster; large projecting ears; the mouth open, and holding two balls in place of teeth; holding in its left hand (perhaps) a stick; each leg terminating in a brush. Size, $1\frac{1}{4}$ inch wide, 2 inches high. Weight, 9 dwt. 9 grs.

No. 8. The head of a bull, having large flat plates projecting from the nostrils, and ornamental scroll-work above the head on each side. Size, $1\frac{1}{4}$ inches wide, $1\frac{3}{8}$ inches high. Weight, 10 dwt. 4 grs.

No. 9. A bird with outspread wings and tail; having an eagle-like head, with curved beak and large projecting eyes, and surmounted by two long crooked horns. Size, $2\frac{1}{2}$ inches wide, $2\frac{1}{8}$ inches high. Weight, 1 oz. 7 dwt. 16 grs.

In connection with these specimens, I have thought that the following account might prove interesting to the members of the Society, even if not new to all of them.

For such information as I have been able to obtain respecting them, I am indebted to a volume entitled, "Antiquarian, Ethnological and other Researches, &c., &c.," by William Bollaert, F.R.G.S., London, 1860, and to papers by F. M. Otis, M.D., and by Mr. E. G. Squier, published in Harper's Weekly, in 1859.

That these relics date back to a very early period, there

seems to be but little doubt, not only from the fact that the present Indian tribes of Central America have no knowledge of these huacas, nor of the art of making the images found in them, but in the " History of New Granada" by Col. Joachin Acosta, mention is made of a discovery by the Spaniards as far back as the 15th century of similar treasures at Zenu, in the Province of Antiochia, New Granada. After speaking of the discovery of the riches in the Indian burial-grounds at Zenu, the historian proceeds with the following description : " The cemetery of Zenu was composed of an indefinite number of mounds of earth, some of a conical form, and others more or less square. When an Indian died, it was the custom to dig a hole capable of containing his arms and jewels, *which were placed on the left hand side of his grave, looking towards the east*, and around these were placed earthen vases containing chichi and other fermented drinks ; also Indian corn, and stones to pound the same ; also his wives and slaves (if he was a principal man), which last, thoroughly intoxicated themselves previously to the interment ; and then the whole was covered over with a species of red earth brought from a distance. Then the mourning commenced, which lasted as long as there remained any thing to drink, and in the meanwhile the mourners continued to throw earth upon the grave ; thus it was elevated according to the ability of the individual or family to provide a greater or less quantity of liquor. Jewels of gold in large or small quantities were found in all the tombs. In some were golden figures representing every class of animals from man to the ant, and sometimes in amount to the value of ten, twenty, and even thirty thousand dollars."

They all have little rings at their backs for suspension ; and were doubtless designed as pendants either for the nose or ears, or were to be worn on the breast of their ancient owner. Farther to the southward, in Peru, the aborigines were remarkably skillful in working the precious metals. They cast them in moulds, soldered them, inlaid them, and reduced them into leaves. They were generally cast hollow, and with such perfection as often to leave no trace of the joints of the mould.

They sometimes cast objects combining gold, silver, and copper, in alternate bands, so well inlaid and united as to appear to form one mass. Occasionally in vases and other open vessels, they embossed figures on the outside by hammering from the interior.

In the latter part of June, 1859, a native of Bugalita, a small town in the district of Boqueron, in the province of Chiriqui, (New Granada), while wandering through the forest in the vicinity of his cabin, encountered a tree which had been prostrated by a recent tempest, and underneath its upturned roots he espied a small earthen jar. Upon examination this proved to contain, wrapped in swathing of half decayed cloth, divers images of curious and fantastic shape, and of so yellow and shining a metal, that he at once suspected them to be gold. Knowing himself to be in the midst of an ancient Indian "huaca," or burial ground, he immediately commenced an exploration of the little burial mounds which were on every side, very shrewdly suspecting that they also might contain treasures of a like character.

The result was, that in a very short time, (three or four days), he succeeded in exhuming no less than seventy-five pounds weight of these images. Not exactly confident, however, of the quality and value of the metal, he disclosed to his neighbors his discovery; and in less than a fortnight over a thousand people were at work, having dug up "more than nine arrobas," (225 pounds weight) of images, most of which proved to be of the finest gold. This is the substance of the information in regard to the discovery of these ancient relics, brought to the city of Panama by two natives of Bugalita, who substantiated their statements by bringing also with them, in their canoe, seventy-five pounds' weight of golden images for sale. They also reported that there had been so great an excitement among the inhabitants for many miles around the huacas, that towns and flourishing estates were wholly deserted ; and that, in consequence of so great and unexpected an influx into that region, there had already come to be a great dearth of provisions, and that considerable suffering had been the consequence.

The Governor of Chiriqui, in a letter to the Governor of Panama, stated that considerably more than $100,000 worth of images had been taken up; that over 4,000 graves had been rifled, and that as there were innumerable graves in the vicinity still untouched, there was little doubt but that immense wealth would be eventually realized therefrom.

The portion of the treasure which had been received at Panama, consisted of small images of gold, which had evidently first been cast in clay moulds, and afterwards hammered to the requisite degree of smoothness. The workmanship of many exhibited no little mechanical skill and ingenuity. Quite a large proportion were of virgin gold, while others varied in purity from 15 to 20 carats fine, owing undoubtedly to the artificers being ignorant of the art of separating the baser metals from the gold in its native state. The most frequent alloy was of copper.*

Objects found in the tombs made of gold of low standard or alloyed with copper, were called guanin, or gianin and tumbaga;† this class of metal was known as far as Honduras; its sp. gr. is 11·55. It was assayed in Spain, and found to consist of 63 gold, 14 silver, and 9 copper. A recent analysis of gold from Titiribi᷃ in Columbia, gave gold 76·41, silver 23·12, and copper 0·3. In size these images varied from 3 pennyweights to 6 ounces, representing wild beasts, birds, fishes, reptiles, and semi-human monsters, hideous to the last degree;

* "Life of Columbus," by Irving, ii., 177. In 1503, Columbus, when on the Mosquito coast, says, "there was no pure gold to be met with here, all their ornaments were of guanin; but the natives assured us that in proceeding along the coast, the ships would soon arrive at a country where gold was in abundance. On the coast of Veragua, the Spaniards met with specimens of pure gold for the first time; the natives wearing large plates of it suspended around their necks by cotton cords; they had likewise ornaments of guanin, gold of low standard, an alloy with copper, or a natural metal, rudely shaped like eagles."

† Velasco, i., 31. Tumbaga or pucacuri (bad gold), is an alloy of gold and copper. It is found in a natural state in the mines of Patia de Popayan and Villonaco de Loja. This guanin is first mentioned by Columbus as forming the ornament of a chief, when coasting along the south side of Jamaica, in 1494.

in very many, if not all the graves were found three plates of gold, from three to twelve inches in diameter, each pierced near the centre by two holes. But little reliable information could be gathered as to the condition in which the graves and their contents were found, except that on the left hand side of every grave, looking toward the east, were the jars containing one or more golden images.

According to Mr. E. G. Squier, the discovery of these relics is earlier than above stated; he says in 1859 that "large quantities have been taken out from time to time, for many years past; and I was informed by the late Governor of the Bank of England, that several thousand pounds worth were annually remitted from the Isthmus, as bullion, to that establishment," he adds, "as to the origin and date of these relics there is no doubt." Columbus when he discovered Chiriqui Lagoon, in his fourth voyage, found all the chiefs and important people decorated with these and similar ornaments, which, as he says in his relation, gave him "great promise of the richness of the country in gold and silver." Hence he named the district Castilla del Oro; and hence the coast came to be known as Costa Rica, or rich coast, a name still preserved, as that of the State of Central America adjoining the Isthmus. He mentions particularly among the ornaments worn by the chiefs, great plates or mirrors of gold suspended on their breasts, "which they would neither sell nor exchange." These plates were from three to twelve inches in diameter. Columbus adds that the Indians cast gold with some degree of skill, "but in no way equal to the Spaniards." He says, also, that "in all the regions around Veragua, the Indians inter with their chiefs, when they die, all the gold which they possess."

REMARKS

ON

TABASCO, MEXICO,

OCCASIONED BY

THE REPORTED DISCOVERY OF REMAINS OF ANCIENT CITIES BEING FOUND IN THAT LOCALITY.

A PAPER READ BEFORE

"The Numismatic and Antiquarian Society of Philadelphia,"

THURSDAY EVENING, APRIL 5, 1866,

BY

CHARLES H. HART,

CORRESPONDING SECRETARY.

PHILADELPHIA:

1867.

REMARKS ON TABASCO, MEXICO.

I HAVE no doubt but that other gentlemen present, as well as myself, noticed in the daily papers about two weeks since, the following paragraph: "Ancient Cities Discovered. The Department of State, has received dispatches from our Consul at Tabasco, Mexico, dated January 3, 1866, in which he communicated the discovery of the ruins of two ancient cities, which have remained unknown since the days of the Conquest. The first, he says, from its topography and situation, he is led to believe is one occupied by Cortez, at the time of his invasion of Tabasco, and is situated about fifteen miles to the west of Frontera, a town at the mouth of Tabasco or Grijalva river; the other is situated in the north-eastern portion of the State, nearly opposite the present city of Laguna de los Terminos, and was known before the Conquest as Xicolanca. The traditions connected with it trace its origin to a period at least two hundred years before the Christian era."

Having a desire to learn more of these interesting archæological remains for the purpose of laying it before the Society, I addressed the Honorable Secretary of State, soliciting a copy of the original dispatch, and speedily received a very complimentary letter in reply, enclosing the desired information. I now read it from the official copy.

UNITED STATES COMMERCIAL AGENCY,
Tabasco, January 3, 1866.

SIR :

* * * I have to inform the Department, that in my explorations in this State, I have discovered the ruins of two ancient cities, which have remained unnoticed and unknown since the days of the Conquest. The first from its situation and the topography of the surrounding country, I am led to believe is the same that Cortez occupied at the time of his invasion of

Tabasco. The edifices, though in complete ruins, afford proof and incontestible evidence of the vastness and grandeur of the ancient capitol of Tabasco, which before the Conquest was called Ccutla, and is situated about fifteen miles to the west of Frontera, a town at the mouth of the Tabasco or Grijalva river. The other is situated in the north-eastern part of the State, nearly opposite the present city of Laguna de los Ter- minos, and was known before the Conquest as Xicolanea, and the traditions connected with it, trace its origin to a period at least two hundred years before the Christian era.

I regretted that the condition of my health was such as to prevent me from prosecuting investigations which might have contributed something illustrative of the history of the ancient civilized nations of Mexico. However, the result of my obser- vations will be given to the world in a work which I design publishing during the coming year, on Mexico. I may add that the present sites of these cities are the pictures of desola- tion, and can with truth be called "howling wildernesses."

The vast district of country lying between Gautemala and Mexico, in the vicinity of the great lake of Pelew-Itsa, has never been explored, and now that peace has again blessed our country, we might cause the whole to be explored, together with the sources of Usumasinta, which here are as great a mystery as the sources of the Nile.

I remain sir, very respectfully your obedient servant,

B. W. SANDERS.

To Hon. WM. H. SEWARD,
    Washington City.

In acknowledging the receipt of the above document, I inquired for the postal address of Mr. Sanders, intending to correspond with him on the subject, but was informed " that he had ceased to be connected with the Department, and that of his present whereabouts it was not informed." Thinking it might be of interest to the Society to hear something, but little it is true, of the locality of these remains and the events hap- pening there at the time of the Conquest, I have drawn the following account from the old chroniclers.

Juan de Grijalva, who has the glory of being the first navi- gator to set foot on Mexican soil, sailed from St. Jago de Cuba, on the fifth of April, 1518, according to Bernal Diaz, although by Herrera and De Solis, it was three days later, and Prescott,

who gleans it from a MSS. copy of the "Itinerary" of the commander's chaplain, says it was on the first of the succeeding
May, in command of a squadron of four vessels fitted out by
Don Diego Velasquez, Governor of the Island, for the purpose
of further exploring those countries upon which, the adventurer
Cordova had been driven in a heavy storm, and which he
reported to be a land "where the houses were built of lime
and stone and the inhabitants decently clad ; that they showed
maize, and possessed gold."

After having been absent a little more than a month, taking
Diaz, who was of the expedition for my guide, they entered
the river Tabasco, which was then christened the Grijalva in
honor of their captain, and held an amicable conference with
a chief, who presented Grijalva "with divers curiosities of
more workmanship than value," says De Solis, "and plumes
of various colors, robes of fine cotton, with some figures of animals to adorn them, made of gold, thin and light, or curiously
wrought in wood, set in gold or overlaid with it." Antonio de
Herrera, and others who follow him, affirms that the Cazique
presented Grijalva with a suit of armor of fine gold with all
the pieces belonging to it ; that he armed himself completely
with them, and that they fitted him as well as if they had been
made for him.

Grijalva having visited various other parts of this new found
land, and thinking himself successful beyond his most sanguine
expectations, returned to Cuba after an absence of nearly six
months, when he was surprised to find that another and much
larger armament was being fitted out to follow up his own discoveries, accounts of which had been received from Alvarado,
who was dispatched with advices to the Governor.

This second expedition was placed under the command of
Hernando Cortez, a Hidalgo, native of Medellin in Estrema-
dura, born according to the most trustworthy sources in the
year 1485, although Orellana says "that Cortez came into the
world the same day that that *infernal beast, the false heretic
Luther* entered it," which was two years earlier than I have
given. He was consequently in his thirty-fourth year when

7

this important commission was placed in his hands, and parting with all his property, the better to provide for the fleet, he went rapidly to work, in order to fit out his squadron with the least possible delay, and set sail from St. Jago in the still of the night of the 18th November, 1518; directed his course to Trinidad and other towns on the Island, for the purpose of recruiting volunteers for his ships, and finally on the eighteenth day of February, 1519, he weighed anchor and made for the coast of Yucatan. Stopping on the way at Cozumel, he arrived on the thirteenth of March at the mouth of the Tabasco or Grijalva river, and the large ships not being able to pass the bar, came to anchor.

The Spaniards were at once struck with the appearance of boats filled with Indians, some armed, and all much superior in aspect to those of the Islands. Leaving a sufficient force to guard the ships, Cortez embarked the rest in brigatines and small boats with several pieces of artillery, and rowed up the river against a strong current. When he had proceeded a little more than half a league, he discovered a large town "with houses built of sun-dried bricks, and covered with thatched roofs." It was surrounded by a wall of timber, of great strength and provided with loopholes, through which arrows, stones and darts were discharged in time of war. "The compass," says De Solis, "was round, without any traverses or other defences, and at the closing of the circle, the extremity of one line covered the other, and formed a narrow winding street, in which were two or three little castles of wood, which filled up the passage, and wherein they were used to post their sentinels; a sufficient fortress against the arms of this new world, where they were happily ignorant of the arts of war, and of those methods to attack and defend in which mankind have been instructed, either by malice or necessity."

Accosting some of the canoes through the interpreter Aguilar, Cortez requested leave to land for supplies of fresh water and provisions, of which they were in want, and would pay well. The boatmen promised to take a message to the town and bring an answer. They went, and soon returned bringing five or six boats "filled with bread, and a few turkeys," which they told the Spaniards to accept as a gift. Cortez replied that these were entirely inadequate to their wants, on account of the number of persons in the large ships below, which they had not seen, and he begged they would send word to allow him to enter the town and obtain his supplies. The Indians asked one night to consider his request, and retired to the town, while Cortez went to a small island in the river, where he waited till morning for their answer.

Both parties practiced some deception, the Indians wanting the time to carry their effects and women and children away to the mountains, and to rally their warriors, while Cortez sent for the remainder of his force which had been left in the vessels, to come up to the island, and caused a search to be made in the river for a fording place. Neither side was aware of the action of the other. The men came up from the ships, and a ford was found within less than half a mile above, where the water was only two or three feet deep ; they also discovered a thicket of trees, under shelter of which they could approach very near the town without being seen. Cortez, on obtaining this information, immediately directed his officers, Alonzo de Avila and Pedro de Alvarado, with each one hundred men, to occupy the woods the same night, so as to be in readiness, on hearing a signal, to attack the town on the land side in the morning. This place where Avila landed, is called by Diaz "Palmares," and approached Tabasco by a very narrow road. As soon as it was day, eight canoes, crowded with armed men, more numerous than before, came to the island, bringing a very small quantity of provisions, saying that they could not fetch more as the inhabitants had all fled from fear, and they therefore begged that the Spaniards would take this supply and return to sea, and not disturb the peace of the country. The interpreter answered that it was shameful to leave them to perish with hunger, and that they would soon repent it. They replied that they knew them not, and as they had a "frightful" appearance, they feared to admit them to their houses, and if they wanted water they could take it out of the river or dig wells as they had to do. Cortez then said that he could by no means depart without entering the place and seeing the country, for the purpose of giving an account of it to the greatest lord of the world, who had sent him there, and that they might give him a favorable reception or not, as they pleased, for he would commend himself to the power of God and his own strength.

The natives retorted that he had better go away and not boast in other people's country, and that as to entering the town, they would never permit it, and if attempted, would destroy them all. Cortez still persisted in his endeavors to obtain a friendly reception, but finding it in vain, gave the signal for the attack on the land, and he himself at the head of two hundred men, approached in boats near the town, when he discharged his ordnance and then leaped into the water to the knees and began the assault on the walls. The Indians fought with desperation, wounding several of their opponents with their arrows and darts; and although terrified at the strange noise of the fire-arms, made a courageous resistance, and fled not from the defences. But the land force coming upon them unawares, entered on the side where it was undefended; the Indians seeing this left the river front to defend the other part of the town, and in the meantime Cortez entered, partially barefooted, having left one of his buskins in the mud, and drove the savages before him "up the street to a second barricade, behind which they posted themselves, fronting us (the Spaniards) valiantly, whistling and shouting 'al calcachioni,' or 'kill the captain.'" Bernal Diaz continues, "We now drove the enemy before us, though they fought manfully and never could be made to turn their backs, until they arrived at a great enclosed court, where were some large apartments and halls, and three houses containing idols. Here they collected all their effects, but as they were forced to evacuate this last post, our general ordered a halt, and that they should be pursued no farther." The soldiers searched the place, but found nothing but Indian corn, turkeys, some articles of cotton and a few grains of gold, and Cortez took up his quarters in the temples, which were spacious enough to contain all his followers. This was the first city taken by force of arms in the course of the expedition.

Peter Martyr, in the De Insulis, gives a glowing picture of this Indian capital, the particulars of which he received from the old pilot Alaminos, and from two of the officers of Cortez, who revisited Spain in the course of that year. He says: "Ad fluminis ripam protentum dicunt esse oppidum, quantum non ausim dicere: mille quingentorum passuum, ait Alaminus nauclerus, et domorum quinque ac viginti millium: stringunt alij, ingens tamen fatentur et celebre. Hortis intersecantur domus, quæ sunt *egregiè lapidibus et calce fabrefactæ, maximâ industriâ et architectorum arte.*"

The following morning Cortez sent out a detachment under Alvarado, and another under Francisco de Lugo, to reconnoiter. The latter officer had not advanced a league before he learned the position of the natives, by their attacking him in such force that he was fain to take shelter in a large "stone building," where he was closely beseiged, but the first party coming up, drove the beseigers off, and the combined forces returned to the main body. Cortez learning from a prisoner who had been taken that a large body of Indians were encamped on a level ground a few miles distant from the city, called the plain of Ceutla, determined to attack them the next day, which was Lady-day, the twenty-fifth of March. The horses were ordered to be landed from the ships, and were assigned to the most accomplished horsemen and bravest soldiers, twelve in number, whose names are all indelibly recorded on the pages of Diaz, who further says, Cortez presented each one with a breastplate decorated with bells.

All the necessary dispositions being made the little army heard mass, and then sallied forth for the conflict, the cavalry making a lengthy circuit in order to avoid some marshy ground. The troops advanced more than a league without descrying the enemy, until at length they beheld their dusky lines stretching as far as the eye could reach, along the edge of the horizon. The Indians had shown some sagacity in the choice of their position, and as the weary Spaniards came slowly on, encumbered with their heavy mail, the Tabascians sent up their hideous yells and discharged volleys of arrows, stones and other missiles, which rattled like hail on the shields and helmets of the assailants. Many were wounded before they could gain the firm ground, where they soon cleared a space for themselves, and opened a heavy fire of artillery and musketry on the dense masses of the enemy. Numbers were swept down at every discharge, but the bold barbarians far from being dismayed, threw up dust and leaves to hide their losses, and sounding their war instruments, shot off fresh flights of arrows in return. The Spaniards began to fear they had underated their opponents to too great a degree, and were just on the verge of retiring, when the most distant column of the enemy was seen to be agitated and thrown into disorder, and a few moments later they heard the welcome shouts of "San Jago and San Pedro." The horse had arrived. The savages, terrified at the mountainous apparition of horse and rider, thinking them one and the same, were seized with a panic and fled, leaving the field and victory to the invaders. Many prisoners were taken, among whom were two chiefs or caziques, whom Cortez treated with marked kindness, in order to win them to him.

The captured natives were much struck by the neighing of the horses, and imagining they spoke, inquired of the conquerors what they said, who replied that they were offended on account of their having fought against them. The simple Indians thereupon asked the horses their pardon, and gave them "roses and turkey bones" to eat. De Solis gives the following minute account of the weapons used by the natives in this action, which I think well worth transcribing. "Most of them wear bows and arrows; the bow strings were made of the sinews of beasts or of thongs of deer skins twisted, and their arrows for want of iron were headed with stones ground sharp, or fish bones. They used also a kind of dart which sometimes they threw, and at others they managed like a pike, as occasion required. They had likewise long swords which they used with both hands, as we do our broadswords, made of wood, in which they fixed sharp flints. The strongest of them had clubs, pointed with flints, and there were slingers who threw stones with great force and skill. The defensive arms, which were only used by commanders and persons of distinction, were quiltings of cotton awkwardly applied before the breast, fitted breast-plates, and shields of wood or tortoise shell adorned with plates of such metal as they could get, some making use of gold as we do iron. They had also music with which they animated their soldiers and gave signals, as flutes made of great canes, sea shells; and a sort of drum made of the trunk of a tree, so hollowed and made thin that they answered to the stroke of the stick a very displeasing sound."

The two captured chiefs after being presented with numerous trinkets, were persuaded to return to their friends and exhort them to come into amicable terms. This mission they executed very faithfully, the result of which was that the next day the chiefs of the province sent "fifteen slaves" with their faces besmeared with black and wretchedly clad, in sign of contrition for what had passed. The day following this, thirty Indians of rank in habiliments of state, came bearing presents and to ask permission to bury their dead, "for fear that they would be eaten by the lions and tigers." This being granted them, they proceeded "to burn and inter" the bodies. They also informed Cortez that on the succeeding day he would receive an embassy to treat conclusively of peace. Accordingly at the time mentioned, ten native dignitaries, richly dressed, arrived with much ceremony. They approached with very great submission, and having perfumed him with their vessels of incense, in which were burned according to De Solis, gum anime, gum copal and other sweet scents, a very usual ceremony, when they would express the greatest veneration, they delivered their embassy, praying pardon for their past conduct, and declaring their good intentions for the future. These embassadors were followed by a long train of servants, including the celebrated slave Marina, so baptized by the Spaniards, who finally became the friend and interpreter of Cortez. The next day an altar was built and a crucifix erected, when the town of

Tabasco changed its name to that of *Santa Maria de la Vitoria*, and the following morning being Palm Sunday, after hearing mass, the entire army re-embarked and set sail for St. Juan de Uloa, where they arrived on Holy Thursday.

This, gentlemen, is a summary drawn from all the sources at my command of the doings and actions of the conquerors and the conquered, at the place which has just been brought to our notice by the vigilance of Mr. Sanders, from whom I trust you may all hear soon a much better and more satisfactory account by means of the work he promises in the foregoing letter.

NOTE.—Tabasco is a south-east state of Mexico, extending from latitude 17° to 18° 40′ N., longitude 91° 20′ to 94° 40′ W., and is bounded on the north by the Gulf of Mexico, on the east by Yucatan, on the south by Chiapas and Guatemala, and on the west by the territory of Tehuantepec; it has an area of 15,609 square miles, and a population of about 75,000, chiefly Indians.

SOME CONSIDERATIONS

ON THE

BEST MEANS OF PROMOTING THE EFFICIENCY

AND

EXTENDING THE USEFULNESS

OF THE

𝔑𝔲𝔪𝔦𝔰𝔪𝔞𝔱𝔦𝔠 𝔞𝔫𝔡 𝔄𝔫𝔱𝔦𝔮𝔲𝔞𝔯𝔦𝔞𝔫 𝔖𝔬𝔠𝔦𝔢𝔱𝔶,

OF PHILADELPHIA.

A PAPER READ BEFORE THE SOCIETY AT A STATED MEETING,

Held April 5th, 1866,

By HENRY PHILLIPS, Jr.

PHILADELPHIA:
1867.

SOME CONSIDERATIONS, ETC.

"The inquiry after knowledge is the highest and best aim of the human understanding. The Mahometans hold as a part of their religious creed, that it is their duty to 'search for learning even in the remotest parts of the earth.' "* All wisdom is comparative. There is nothing so obscure of which time may not reveal some use; there is nothing so insignificant or so trifling that may not ultimately prove of paramount importance.

Next to the collection and preservation of learning comes the distribution of it, and the question which I this evening propose to consider, is, "How may our Society most benefit itself and the world at large by the dissemination of the stores of knowledge which it may chance to garner up?"

All objects of Antiquarian Research are germane to our Society, are well known to all of our members, and must appear in so powerful a light, that, but the slightest intimation of them may be necessary. Let our attention be turned for a few moments to the *means* by which we may best accomplish the ends of our corporate existence, and I hope that the assent of the Society may not be withheld from the substance of the crude remarks which I am about to offer for its consideration.

For the support and prosperous workings of an association like our own, contributions of a *literary* nature are most especially requisite.

We deal entirely in abstractions far removed from the tumults of every day life. Our transactions are not with the quick but with the dead of centuries. To our meetings the members can repair, confident that there they will find repose from their ordinary thoughts and pursuits, and that the succession of new

* Sir William Jones.

and diverse ideas will afford relief to their jaded spirits. Our objects are of the nature most suggestive, most important and most prolific of results; nor can the reproach of learned trifling "difficiles nugae" be used with truth against such Societies. "The days have gone by when archæological pursuits were little more than the harmless but valueless recreations of the aged and the idle. The spirit of critical inquiry has separated the gold from the dross, and antiquities are now considered valuable in proportion to their illustration of history or their importance to art."*

The utility of the ends so often gained by similar labors is the best refutation of so stale a charge.

It is the duty, and it should be the pleasure of every member to resolve that in the course of each successive year he would contribute *something* of interest to be placed on the records of the Society. It is of no consequence how brief or how unskillfully composed such a communication might be; for our purposes it amply suffices as an item in the diffusion of knowledge, and as manifesting the interest taken by the members in the progress of the Society.

The Bibliographer might furnish memoranda of rare or curious books seen by him or in his library; notes of editions, collations of authors, descriptions of manuscripts, special bibliographical lists, &c., &c., or anything whatever that has proved of interest to himself.

The collector of Autographs could show the choicest of his treasures, or such special matters as were of value or worthy of permanent preservation.

The Numismatist could describe or exhibit strange or fine coins, medals, or dies, or numismatic works, or anything falling within his special province.

He, to whom the vast Continent of America, with its aboriginal remains and relics, weapons and implements, mounds and palaces, forms the source of interest, might also share with the Society the thoughts that arise in his mind from the contemplation of those vast and venerable records.

* Planché, British Costums, introduction.

The general Archæologist, before whom the whole wide
world lies open, from North to South, from East to West,
might also contribute to the same result.

The Timbrophile, the Heraldic investigator, and all the
varied forms of antiquarianism might be comprehended thus
within our scope.

Let the rule be established, "That whatever interests any
one member in his individual archæological pursuits, is also
of interest to the Society, and that the Society will with pleasure receive at all times any additions, however slight to its
stock of knowledge."

Let each member think within himself, if there is no question in all the domain of Archæology which he would like to
have answered or discussed. If such query were presented at
a meeting of the Society it would either then and there be discussed and satisfactorily settled, or else referred, to be in the
future, investigated.

Our standing committees on Numismatics and on Antiquities
should exert themselves to procure questions for the consideration of the Society. To them should be referred all such in-
terrogations as, in the opinion of the Society, should appear worthy of a full investigation, and these Committees, if it
seemed best to them, should request such member or members
of the Society to whom the subject was most familiar, or its
treatment could be most profitably committed, to prepare a
suitable response.

In this manner we should possess with no great labor and by
imperceptible degrees a vast amount of knowledge germane and
proper to our organization. Our corresponding members might
be solicited for literary contributions, and apprised from time
to time of our toils and of our success.

No harm could result from such an experiment, and much
good might ensue.

Nor need a stimulus to effort be wanting. If it should be
feared that an appeal in favor of the intellectual prosperity of
the Society might fail in its effect, let us have recourse to a
commoner motive. *Emulation* in our pursuits would be a

healthy feeling. Let us encourage and foster it by awarding annually at our January meeting a medal to be struck from dies the property of the Society, to the member who has prepared and read before or transmitted to the Society during the past year, the best original paper or essay on subjects kindred to our scope.

As a rough suggestion I would throw out that if such dies or funds necessary for their purchase were presented to the Society by any one member, such medal could be called " The ———— prize," and be a cheap immortality. The conditions under which it might be competed for could easily be arranged by the Society.

These are but rough germs of thought which, however, are respectfully submitted to the Society, in the hope that under its hand they may ripen into perfection.

MEDICINE AND ASTROLOGY.

A PAPER READ BEFORE

THE NUMISMATIC AND ANTIQUARIAN SOCIETY

OF PHILADELPHIA,

ON THURSDAY EVENING, JUNE 7, 1866.

By HENRY PHILLIPS, Jr.

PHILADELPHIA:
1867.

MEDICINE AND ASTROLOGY.

In presenting to night to the Library of our Society a curious and rare work upon the above subject, I cannot but think that a succinct account of the book and its contents may prove of interest.

The belief in astrology is among the earliest superstitions that possessed the human race, and that it should be so, seems natural, when we reflect that mankind's first condition was nomadic in its nature; that forced to dwell in the open air the contemplation of the natural phenomena which surrounded it, and of the celestial portents and prodigies of such wonderful occurrence in their regularities and in their changes, soon led to a belief in the connection of the heavenly bodies with terrestrial affairs, and to a credence in the influence exerted by them upon the destinies of man. And those who arrogated to themselves the superior position in the rude communities of primitive times united in themselves all knowledge such as then was possible to be obtained, and claiming power to read in the stars the fate of the world, demanded also, that they should be believed to have such revelations therefrom as were of beneficial nature. The belief in the influence of the celestial bodies is a pleasing one, as it, by depriving man of his free will, must also deprive him of his responsibility, and to a lucky or unlucky star must be charged what otherwise might be accounted for in some less satisfactory manner. Granted that a constellation or certain conjunction of the heavens ruled at the native's birth, it was necessary to believe that the circumstances portended by such an occurrence would also accompany him throughout his existence. That, therefore, when any thing befell such a one, it was necessary to know his past astrological life in order to know his future, whether for good or for ill.

Burton in his Anatomy of Melancholy declines to discuss the

8

question as he expresses it, as to whether " Sextus Empiricus, Picus Mirandula, Sextus ab Heminga, Pererius, Erastus, Chambers, &c., have so far prevailed with any man that he will attribute no virtue at all to the heavens, or to sun or moon, more than he doth to their signs at an inn keeper's post or tradesman's shop," and gives as his opinion " that the stars incline but not compel." Doubtless his opinion was that which the learned of his day professed, and the remark of Kepler, that " astrology, though a fool was a daughter of a wise mother, to whose support and life the foolish daughter was indispensable,"* contributed yet still to preserve its credit, and even as late as 1705, so little was it thoroughly eradicated from common belief, that the editor of " Les Connaissance des Tems," found it necessary to apologize for the absence of all predictions in that astronomical work, stating the academy had never recognized the solidity of the rules given by the ancients for discovering the future by the configuration of the stars. Although the superstition has long since been driven away by the steady advance of civilization, so that its existence is but precarious even in the hearts of the ignorant and degraded, its traces are indelibly stamped upon the every day language, even of the most educated classes, and our best literature may be found full of words and phrases left by the subsiding waves of error.

" Old errors," says Trench,† " dismissed long ago, may survive in language, being bound up in words that grew into use when those errors found credit, and which now that those errors are dismissed, maintain still their currency among us. * * * * * * No one now believes in astrology, that the planet under which a man may happen to be born will affect his temperament, will make him for life of a disposition grave or gay, lively or severe. Yet we seem to affirm as much in language, for we speak of one as *jovial* or *saturnine* or *mercurial;* 'jovial' as being born under the planet Jupiter or Jove, which was the joyfullest star, and of happiest augury of all; a gloomy severe person is said to be 'saturnine,' as

* Brande's Encyc.   † Trench on the Study of Words.

born under the planet Saturn, who was considered to make those that own his influence, and were born when he was in the ascendant, grave and stern as himself; another we call 'mercurial,' or light hearted, as those born under the planet Mercury were accounted to be. The same faith in the influence of the stars still survives in 'disastrous,' 'ill starred,' 'ascendency,' 'lord of the ascendant,' and indeed in 'influence' itself."

These are but a very few instances which I will not prolong farther, that I may not commit too great a trespass upon the valuable time of the learned gentlemen who to-night are so kindly granting me their attention.

The title of the work that has induced these few remarks is as follows :—

De ratione et usu dierum criticorum opus recens natum, in quo mens tum ipsius Ptolemœi, tum aliorum astrologorum hac in parte dilucidatur. Authore, Thoma Boderio Rhotomagensis Diœcesis. Cui accessit Hermes Trismegistus de decubitu infirmorum, nunquam anteà in lucem editus. Parisiis, in officina Audœni Parvi ad Lilii insigne, via Jacobæa. Anno Salutis, M. D. L. V. Small 4to. p. 57.

Which title may be thus translated :

" A new book on the doctrine and use of critical days in which the system of Ptolemy and other astrologers is illustrated and explained, by Thomas Boderius, of the diocese of Rouen ; to which is added a work never before published, by Hermes Trismegistus, on the bed keeping of the sick. Paris, at the warehouse of Owen Pettit, at the sign of the Lily, Rue Jacob. Anno Domini, 1555."

Upon the title page is a rude wood-cut device of the printer, representing the letters O. P., above a lily in a shield supported by two lions rampant, while on a scroll above is the motto *Petit a petit.* The whole is a play upon words ; the letters O. P. being the initial of the publisher's name, the lily being the sign of his shop, and the motto being a pun upon his name.

On the last page we find the following :—

Parisiis, excudebat Andreas Wechelus, sub Pegaso, in vico Bellovaco, Anno Salutis, 1555.

The work is dedicated to Orontius Finèus, (Oronce Finè,) Professor of Mathematics in the Royal College at Paris. A preface follows, in the course of which the author mentions his being advanced in years, after which then as was often the custom, appears a page of epigrams in Greek and Latin laudatory of Doctor Boderius and his work.

But scanty information is extant to us respecting this author, but he is known to have been a physician of Rouen. The book must be rare as I have never met with it in any foreign catalogue through which I have searched, nor have I ever seen or heard of another copy.

I translate a few of the opening sentences, so as to present some general idea of the scope of the book.

" Part first, concerning the doctrine of critical days, wherein is for the first time made known, how very necessary the knowledge of astrology is to a physician."

" After beginning by setting forth our premises, we subjoin the words of Hippocrates, than whom no one is greater among the chiefs of the physicians, where in his treatise " de crisi et hora decumbentium," he says : Of what nature can he be, that doctor who is not familiar with astrology ? Let no man trust himself into the hands of such, for he is not a thorough physician ; he is like unto a blind man who searcheth his way with a staff, nor the adornment of the physician's name doth he deserve. Nor can any man be skilled in medicine who knoweth not the times and ways of the heavenly bodies and of the influences which the moon exerciseth upon the human frame. * * * * * * He who plyeth the healing art unversed in natural magic or practical astrology, his soul, saith Galen, wandering perpetually in darkness will wax old ; not only doth he fail in rectitude, but in verity may he be called a deceiver. Moreover, if he hath diligently considered the hour of sickness, and hath by laboring in his vocation received its fullest fruits, then truly will it be granted to him to know and to foretell the issue of the disease ; for Galen saith we should inquire the figure of the patient's geniture ; all which things we may thoroughly learn from astronomy, by the acknowledgment of all men. Now, resolve in thy soul how very much this most noble art is needful to the true physician ; * * * * * for as Hermes saith that after God the sun and the moon are the life of all that liveth."

The work then goes on in a similar strain, being broken up into many chapters of natures like the following :

" Why the Seventh day is that of the best event."

" Why he who practiseth this art should carefully seek to know the hour wherein the patient took to bed."

" How if the true hour of the sickness escapeth the physician, the sick man dieth."

" Wherefore certain days are critical."

" Of the angels who are our guardians, and the ministers and workers of the mandate of the divine providence."

" Of the seven rulers of the world," viz : Saturn, Jupiter, Mars, the Sun, Venus, Mercury, and the Moon.

"Of special and general matters known by astrology," as for example, the influence of the moon on mankind ; how, when she waxeth, men's bodies become full of humours, and when the wane arriveth, they become againe void : how, therefore, the course of the moon should be regarded as it relateth to the sick. So generally Venus is taken to regard womenfolk, Mercury the Lord of the Seventh House wisdom, the Sun dignities and honors."

"Whence come the intercalary days."

" Of the very great power of Hylecq and Alcocodem."

"Much faith must we hold in Hylecq, the giver of life ; and Alcocodem, he who bringeth on length of years."

"Given the geniture of the patient and the years since Hylecq and Alcocodem to determine the event of the disease."

" Sixteen rules for determining the critical days from the use of the following table," which consisteth in a Ptolemœian Zodiack divided into sixteen parts. And the first part closes with an astrological table, ANTISCIA, in Signis, Gradibus, &c., &c.

The second part is upon the practical usages of the knowledge of critical times, showing the days when he that has sickened must die and those whereon he may recover. It is chiefly taken up with astrological schemes, of which there are fifty-seven, and their explanations, which doubtless were of great value in their time; as, "The moon when she shineth from the lord of the ascendant unto him of the eighth house, beareth death." Yet not alway, for when the disease is of a chronic nature, the sign is not absolutely fatal. "The lord of the ascendant on the eighth house, in conjunction with Mars or Saturn, sheddeth death." These horoscopes are those of patients to whom Dr. Boderius had been professionally called in, and this was his record of their diseases, diagnoses, treatment and results. We transcribe one as a curiosity.

"Nicholas De Camp was taken ill with a most severe sickness on the 16th day of June, 1554, about the 9th hour of the morning. Although phlebotomy was practised at the command of the attending physician, yet did he take no relief, but after the moon had changed her place the disease altered, and after a severe illness and great danger of life, the patient recovered. Be ye therefore heedful of this, when the moon is in a good position in critical times, and those days bring no relief, they portend judgment of death, a long sickness or change of disease."

The second part closeth with an apostrophe to the readers of the book, and surely those who have read it through deserve to be congratulated for their pains. He tells them that much as he respects the great names of Ptolemy and Aben Esra yet all the things he advances are not vain and empty speculations, but those which he has put to the proof and tried, and all the things he recommends are those which in a long practice he has found to be thoroughly reliable. "Quemadmodum hoc in opere satis a me demonstratum est, hujusce rei experientia fidem faciet: ego nisi fuissem gravis annis et ætate jam confecta, non ante annos novem fuissem in lucem editurus nam et adjecturus eram, ea quoque qua experentia comperissem, sed volui aliis fenestram aperire et (ut vetere proverbio dicitur) glaciem scindere; * * * * * * quicquid a me scriptum est lubens submitto judicio ecclesiae et doctorum."

Unwilling that his learning should perish with him, the old man offers his experience to a subsequent generation. Had he not been stricken with years he would not have come forward as an author, but he wished for others to open the window and to rend asunder the obstructions to a free passage of the light.

No doubt he was an intensely regular physician; but not of that school who prescribed "powdered moles when burnt to ashes," "hairs from the bellies of skinks," (whatever they were), "mummy," and other horrible and barbarous expedients. Dr. Boderius was of the school similar to that of the barber in the Arabian nights, who perpetually ceased to exercise his tonsorial craft in order to take observations of the sun, and to tell his unfortunate customer what he supposed the issue of his adventures might be.

I fancy I should place more implicit confidence in my physician if he were to consult the pharmacopœia, than if he were thoroughly conversant with all the astrological books that ever were published.

NOTE.—The celebrated Dr. Erasmus Darwin seems to have held some belief in the effect of extra terrestrial influences, as will be observed from the following passage, noticed by me since reading the above :

"The periodic returns of so many diseases coincide with the diurnal, monthly and annual rounds of time; that any one who would deny the influence of the sun and moon on the periods of the quotidian, tertian and quartan fevers, must deny their effect on the tides and on the seasons." Zoonomia, (Edit. 1796,) vol. ii. p. 510.

THE

DIARY OF JOHN PEMBERTON,

FOR THE YEARS 1777 AND 1778.

.

EDITED FROM THE MSS. IN THE POSSESSION OF THE SOCIETY,

BY

ELI K. PRICE.

A Paper read before "The Numismatic and Antiquarian Society of Philadelphia," Thursday Evening, July 5, 1866.

THE DIARY OF JOHN PEMBERTON.

The Society has referred to me two "Diaries of John Pemberton, for 1777 and 1778," asking me to edit them for publication. These are chiefly interesting as being in the veritable handwriting of one of the most worthy men of his time, at a most interesting period of our history. They are notes made in "Poor Will's Pocket Almanack," printed by Joseph Cruikshank. The first begins thus: "John Pemberton's. My dear mother died 24th of 2d mo., 1765, in her 74th year." 1777, January, 1st mo., "15th, cousin M. Pleasants, d. d. of a daughter." "16th, 17th, 18th, very cold. 19th Oronoake's wife d. d. of a son." "21st, Mark Miller and Thos. Redman, committed to Gloucester Goal, for reading an Epistle in the Meetings." "30th, Hannah Logan, widow of William, died about 6 this morning." Feby. 2d mo., "23d. Saml. Class buried; 24th, snowed all day and is very deep." March, 3d mo., "10th. Jos. White died; 12th, Jos. White buried at the Falls." June "25th, Dr. Young buried." August, 8 mo., "4, 5, 6, 7, 9th, exceeding hot;" 10, 11, 12, 13, 14, 15th, continued very hot." "14th, several persons died suddenly with the heat and drinking cold water. The widdow Morrisson buried, aged about 84; sister to John Bringhurst dec'd; lived about 40 years in the house she died in. 15th, Thos. Tilbury buried. He died last night about 11 o'clock, the effect of drinking water when hot; was down stairs about 6 o'clock in the evening." September, 9 mo., "2d. I was deprived of my liberty, and taken into confinement by order of Congress, and the President and Council of Penna. without any just cause, as were divers other *Friends*. 11th, a bloody battle between the American and English near Birmingham Meeting House.

About same time myself and 19 others banished from Philadelphia as the above was fought, viz., about 5 o'clock, P. M. 20th, English entered and took possession of Philadelphia without opposition. 29th, arrived at Winchester. Our Yearly Meeting held very peaceably at Philadelphia." October, 10th mo., "16th. Elizth. Shipley died, aged about 87 years. 23d, Augusta ship of war blown up. The report reached to Nottingham and shook the windows as Friends sat in Meeting. 10th mo. 24th. Houses at Winchester illuminated on account of the defeat and capture of Genl. Burgoyne and his army." November, 11th mo., "21st. The Americans set fire to their armed vessels in the Delaware. 22d. An earthquake at Philada. between 7 and 8 o'clock, A. M., felt at West river in Ml'd. 28, 29, 30th. Snowed at Winchester, from 9 to 16 inches deep." December, 12th mo., "5th. Esther White died, aged about 77 years. 12th. Snowed in the morning. 25th. Snowed in the morning. 28. Snow about 4 inches deep. 29th. Very cold. 30, 31st. Very cold."

1778. Several money transactions with his brother-in-law, Isaac Zane, Jur., erased as settled. Jany., 1st mo., "4, 5, 6th. Exceeding moderate fine weather, and all the remainder of the week mild, like spring. The 7th, it rained; 11th, much snow; 12th, a fine day, mild; 13th, clear and cold; 14, 15, and 16th, cold; 17th, rainy, snow last night; 23d, very stormy and cold, and snowed; 24th, mild and fine day." February, 2d mo., "8th, deep snow; 9th, fair and very cold; 24, 25th, very mild weather; 27th, snowed much the fore part of the day, mild the latter part; 28th, snowed this morning." March, 3rd mo., "2d. A deep snow. Thos. Gilpin died about 1 o'clock in the morning. 3d. More snow and very cold, T. Gilpin buried." (He was one of the exiles.) "4th, very cold. 8th, a fine day; 9 and 10th, rainy weather. 16th, removed from Winchester to David Brown's. 22d. John Hunt's leg amputated." (He was one of the exiles.) "25th. J. Hunt's leg opened and dressed. 27th, cold and raw day; 28th, fair and pleasant; 29th, very snowy and stormy." April, 4th mo., "21st. Myself and H. D. (Henry Drinker,) left Winchester; 25th, arrived at

Lancaster; 27th, discharged by council; 30th, returned from banishment to Philadelphia." May, 5th mo., "20th. My riding mare brought 2 foles, both mares; one died immediately, and the other in 2 days after. 20th. Phineas Pemberton, brother James's son, died about 7 o'clock, A. M. 21st. Do., buried in the evening." June, 6th mo., "6th. The King's Commissioners, to treat of an accommodation with America arrived. Ship from London also, with provisions for poor Friends, &c. 17th and 18th, the English evacuated Philada., and the Americans entered on the 18th. In the morning, and following days the weather extremely hot, from about the 15th to the beginning of the 7th month, and for some weeks in that, at times very hot, more so than for many years." September, 9th mo., "26th. Yearly Meeting very large; and all the following week very fine weather." October, 10th mo., "5th. Yearly Meeting ended about 7 o'clock, P. M. 9th. Jona. Zane died about 1 o'clock, A. M. 25th. Sister M. Pemberton died, aged about 75. 27th. M. P. buried." November, 11th mo., "4th. John Roberts and Abraham Carlile put to death in this city. 18th. Reese Meredith buried." December, 12th mo., "5th. Rainy. A. Wright put to death. 8, 9th. Clear mild weather. Very cold the latter part of the month; and raw weather most of the other part of the month."

EXPLANATIONS.

1777, 1 mo., 21st. Miller and Redman, committed for reading Epistles from the Friends' Meeting for sufferings held at Philada., dated 21 of 12th mo., 1776. See, 3 Frd's Miscel'y, 104; and Gilpin's "Exiles in Virginia," p. 282 and 291. This Epistle recalled Friends to their peaceful profession, and discouraged the severance of the connection with Great Britain.

1st mo., 30th. Wm. Logan was son of James, Secretary of Wm. Penn, and Chief Justice and Governor of Pennsylvana.

3d mo., 10. Joseph White was a minister at Falls, Bucks County, (Memorials, 359.)

6th mo., 6. Arrival of Comrs. See, 2 Diary of Revolution, 62. Evacuation Ib., 65.

9th mo., 11. This was the battle of Brandywine, fought at Birmingham Meeting House, which was made a hospital by the British. In view of this I was born, and there first worshipped, and there are our dead of the past generations.

10th mo., 16. Elizth. Shipley, a minister, long resident at Wilmington, widow of Wm. Shipley, [Memls. 371; Smith's His. Del. Co. 501.] She made a religious visit to England with Esther White, in 1743. The New Jersey Gazette of March 11, 1778, for the encouragement of the American cause, published her alleged prophecy, *That this country* should not be conquered by Great Britain. (Moore's Diary of the Revln. 2 vol. 31.)

10th mo., 23. Augusta, ship of war blown up. See an account of the battle at Fort Mifflin; Penn. Arch., v. 708, &c. The Augusta frigate was aground in the Delaware under the fire of Fort Mifflin. From that point Nottingham Meeting was distant over forty miles by an air line, being near the Maryland line, and in the South West corner of Chester County.

12th mo., 5th. Esther White was wife of John White, of Wilmington, an earnest, cheerful minister among Friends, (Meml. 374.)

1778, 10th mo., 25th. Mary Pemberton was wife of John's brother, Israel. Her health was seriously affected by the exile of her husband, as was his by that event and her death; and his followed on 22d of 4th mo., 1779. (Ib. 386, and Frd's Misely. 48.)

11th mo., 4. Brief reports of the trials of Roberts and Carlile are in 1 Dallas, 35 and 39. The charges were aiding and assisting the enemy. The alleged offence of the latter was that he had accepted a power to let people out of the city while in possession of the British, and had taken some salt from persons he termed rebels. The overt acts charged against the former were that he persuaded others to enlist with the enemy, and that he was going to the Head of Elk to communicate with the enemy. Nov. 3d. The Supreme Executive Council refused to reprieve, 11 Col. Reed. 614, and on the next day they were hung. These persons were Friends, but acting entirely on their individual responsibility; and were tried under great prejudice and bias of witnesses and public feeling. 11th mo., 18th. Reese Meredith was a merchant and owner of real estate, including a tract in now 20th Ward, of Philadelphia. When Colonel Washington was here about 1755, R. Meredith saw him as a stranger at the Coffee House, and without introduction invited him to share his hospitality; and thence ensued a lasting friendship. · 2 Watson, 165.

12th mo., 5th. A. Wright, was a laborer, convicted of burglary. The occasion of J. Pemberton's note was, no doubt, his aversion to capital punishments.

The brief diary of John Pemberton affords me an occasion to speak of a family, which was ancient in England before the settlement of Pennsylvania, and which has been well known and been most highly esteemed in all of our Colonial and State history. The descendants are very numerous, but much more in the female branches under other names than that of Pemberton.

A great grandson of James Pemberton, hereafter mentioned, Phineas Pemberton Morris, Esquire, furnishes me with the following extracts made by him in England from Baine's History of Lancashire, vol. iii. p. 561 and 2. "Pemberton is a populous and extensive township, containing the manufacturing village of Lamberhead Green. Adam de Pemberton was living in the reign of Richard 1st., and in 3rd John, his son Alan paid ten marks to have seizin of his lands in Pemberton." "An ancient half-timbered habitation called Pemberton Hall, the abode of the De Pemberton's in the reign of Henry VIII., and subsequently of the Marklands, is now scarcely remembered." "A little west from Ince," says Holland Watson, "this place gave name and seat to an ancient family of which Sir Goddard Pemberton settled at St. Albans, 1615; whose son, Ralph Pemberton, Esquire, was twice Mayor of that place, father of Sir Francis Pemberton, Knight, Lord Chief Justice of both Benches and Privy Counsellor, who died 1697, aged 72. Lewis Pemberton, Esquire, succeeded Sir Goddard in the

Shrievalty of Hertford Shire, for the latter part of 1615 and 1617. Was knighted by James Ist at Burry Hall."

The above named Ralph Pemberton, though probably connected by blood, could not have been the same who came to Pennsylvania in 1683, with his son, Phineas, according to the account of the Pemberton family," which I ascribe to the late James Pemberton Parke, son of Doctor Thomas Parke. He was son of William Pemberton, who May 30th, 1625, took a lease of a cottage at Aspull, in Lancashire, of Roger Hindley, of Hindley Hall, its " crofts or clausures of land, gardens, pastures, feedings," &c., for the three lives of his children, Alice, Margay, and Ralph, and the survivor of them. This Ralph's issue were Phineas and Joseph, the former born 11th mo., 31, 1649–50. *Phineas Pemberton* and his wife, Phœbe, came with his aged father, Ralph, who died in 1687, and her father, James Harrison, to Pennsylvania in 1683, and settled at the Falls, in Bucks County. He was a member of Council in 1685, and Speaker of the Assembly in 1698. (1 Col. Records, 125, 548). In him was concentrated several of the most important offices of Bucks County; and the records yet there, which I have seen, abundantly attest his care, neatness, and skill. In 1683, he was appointed deputy Register; in 1686, was appointed deputy Master of the Rolls; in 1689, was appointed Receiver of Proprietary Quit Rents; in 1691, Register General of that County; and in 1696, was made Master of the Rolls in place of Thomas Lloyd. He was also a Surveyor. (Ib. 514.) He died 1st mo., 1st, 1702. He left few his equal "for wisdom and integrity, and a general service." (7 Friends' Miscellany, 36.) *Israel Pemberton*, his son, was born 12 mo., 20th, 1684–5. He was an apprentice with Samuel Carpenter in this City, and become an eminent and successful merchant, and in many ways publicly useful, as well as in his own religious Society. The Philadelphia Monthly Meeting say in their memorial of him, " Having chosen the fear of the Lord in his youth, and being preserved therein, he established and supported an unblemished character by his justice, integrity, and uprightness in his dealing amongst men, and his mild, steady, and prudent conduct through life. He was a member of this meeting near fifty years, and being well grounded in the principles of truth, of sound judgment and understanding, he approved himself a faithful Elder; adorning our holy profession by a life of meekness, humility, circumspection, and a disinterested regard to the honor of truth; of great use in the exercise of our discipline, being a lover of peace and unity in the church, careful to promote and maintain it; constant in the attendance of meetings, and his deportment therein grave, solid, and reverent, and a true sympathizer with those who were honestly concerned in the ministry; a conspicuous example of moderation and plainness; extensive in his charity and of great benevolence."

The deceased Israel Pemberton left three sons who followed his example, and became eminently useful in their generation; *Israel*, the eldest; *James*, born 6th mo., 26th, 1723, and *John*, born 11th mo., 27th, 1727. *James*, as his father, was a successful merchant; a person of great public usefulness, and an elder in the religious Society of Friend; a manager of the Pennsylvania Hospital, and one of the founders of the Pennsylvania Abolition Society. He died 2d mo., 9th, 1809. *John* Pemberton was also bred a merchant; entered into business for a time; but in 1751, began to speak in the ministry; and the greater part of the residue of his life was devoted in the ministry at home and abroad, many years having been spent in foreign lands; and in Pyrmont, Germany, he closed his valuable life and services on the 31st of the 1st month, 1795. His hand traced the notes before us.

All the Pemberton's above named rendered much valuable service to humanity, in maintaining a peaceful and friendly intercourse with the native Indians; in alleviating the sufferings of the African race; and in maintaining all the humane testimonies of the Society of Friends. They were eminent among men at a period of our American history, when we turn to the Quakers of Pennsylvania, and the contiguous colonies and State for the most pleasing examples of human life.

More certainly than other men did the Friends find within themselves the evidence of our immortal being, and in the vivid

0

realization of the future, were enabled to sink the objects and pursuits of this life into comparative unimportance ; except as they were made available for their immortal happiness. Brissot de Warville, when in this country in 1788, studied them with the head and heart of a philosopher and philanthropist, and in writing of an interview he had had with James Pemberton after the loss of a beloved daughter, said, " The Quakers carry to the borders of the tomb this same tranquility of mind ; and it even forsakes not the women at this distressing moment. This is the fruit of their religious principles, and of a regular, virtuous life. They consider heaven as their country ; and they cannot conceive why death, which conducts them to it should be a misfortune. This habitual serenity does not diminish their sensibility. The respectable Pemberton recounted to me the death of a beloved daughter which happened the day before. I could see the tear steal down his cheek, which a moment's reflection caused to disappear. He loved to speak to me of her virtues and her resignation during her long agony. ' She was an angel,' said he, 'and she is now in her place.' This good father did not exaggerate. You will find in this Society many of these celestial images clothed in serenity ; the symbol of eternal peace and conscious virtue." (7 Frd's Miscellany, 81.)

The note of the banishment to Virginia requires a separate consideration. The Friends sent into exile were among the most eminent for influence and usefulness. There were twenty exiles, and besides the three brothers, Pemberton, first named in the order of Council, there were named therein, Thomas Wharton, Senr., Miers Fisher, Phineas Bond, William Drewet Smith, Owen Jones, Jur., Thos. Gilpin, Elijah Brown, Revd. Thos. Coombe, Thos. Fisher, Saml. Fisher, Henry Drinker, Saml. Pleasants, John Hunt, Charles Jervis, Thos. Pike, William Smith, Charles Eddy, Edward Pennington, and Thos. Affleck. In their protest the signatures of two are thus: William Drewit Smith and Samuel R. Fisher. Those who well understand Friends' views and principles can recur to the events without any disposition to reproach their motives or

character. They were non-combatants in principles; and
consequently bound to abide quietly under the government
existing over them. They can take no part in war, can contribute nothing specifically for its support, consequently can
never be rebels against the powers that be. Generally they
did not desire change; and felt a strong attachment to their
relatives and brethren in religious fellowship in England, and
their feelings of humanity shrank from the horrors of war.
Both John and James Pemberton kept journals during the
Revolution much more ample in expression than the brief facts
now serving us as texts. See 7 Frd's Miscellany, 62, and 8th
do. 58. John, feelingly notices the number of soldiers killed
and wounded, and that fresh men came, many of whom, he
says, appear like reputable farmers. "But the sorrowful
reflections occur in thinking how many wives were likely to
become widows and children fatherless ; and that the spectacles
of misery and mortality which abound, had not a more humb-
ling effect upon the minds of the people." And under date
of 3d mo., 22d, 1777 ; he speaks of proclamations for fasts both
in England and America, and prayers for success in the struggle of arms ; and admitting the necessity to fast from all wrong
things, and to humble ourselves because of the great impiety
and wickedness that abound, and of entreaty that the Lord
might have mercy and pity the people, he proceeds to ask,
"How could it be supposed that we, as a Religious Society,
could comply with such voluntary injunctions, when thereby
Friends in England and Friends here might implore the same
Divine Being for contrary and contradictory things !" (Ib. 63.)

After the passage of acts for test oaths the Friends in their
Yearly Meeting of 1778, adopted the following expression of
their views. "On consideration of what is necessary to be
proposed to Friends on the subject of declaration of allegiance
and abjuration, required by some late laws by the Legislatures
who now preside in Pennsylvania and New Jersey, we are
united in judgment, that, consistent with our religious principles, we cannot comply with the requisitions of those laws,
as we cannot be instrumental in setting up or pulling down any

government; but it becomes us to show forth a peaceable and meek behaviour to all men seeking their good, and to live a sober, useful, and religious life, without joining ourselves with any party in war, or with the spirit of strife and contention now prevailing. And we believe that if our conduct is thus uniform and steady, and our hope fixed on the Omnipotent Arm for relief, He will, in time, amply reward us with lasting peace, which hath been the experience of our Friends in time past, and we hope, of some now under suffering."

In the disposition to oppress Friends Washington never participated, and the Pemberton journals, as well as others, afford ample proof of that fact as well as oral traditions.

But the zeal and earnestness of the patriots of the revolution could neither tolerate opposition nor neutrality; and the spirit of the times demanded victims; and hence Friends were banished to Virginia, and some at home were hung. We can see now, at this distance of time, with more perfect information and free from excitement how needlessly they suffered. True Friends, as certainly they were who were sent into exile, could no more give aid and comfort to the enemy than to the American cause; and if wisely left to their own convictions, they would have been found ministering unto human suffering wheresoever found, and proceeding from whatsoever cause, as has been proved during the late war of the rebellion.

A full narrative with the attesting documents relating to the banishment of Friends, and a few of the Episcopal Church was printed by Thomas Gilpin for the subscribers in 1848, and is in the Philadelphia Library. He was son of Thomas Gilpin who died in exile; and his mother, Lydia, was sister of Samuel R. and Miers Fisher.

The John Hunt who died in exile in Virginia, whose eminent services are often mentioned by others in journals and letters, was an eminent minister among Friends. He sustained the principle and courage of his companions, though himself to fall the second victim, and to die after suffering amputation under the discomforts of banishment from home and family.

The John Hunt who died in Virginia was not the same as

the John Hunt whose notes in the Revolution the Society sent to me. The latter was also a minister in the Society of Friends, who resided at Moorestown, N. J., and lived until 1824, and died, aged 84 years. He began a diary in 1770, which he continued unto the year of his death; to be found in 10th volume of Comly's Friends' Miscellany. The notes sent me belong to the 1st volume of that collection. These supposed prognostics were gloomy in prophecy, and for the period of trial and purgation sad in their realization. With Friends, foreboding visions and anticipated troubles, nature herself seemed to sympathize, or the Almighty to show his displeasure with man by marring his works. These were looked upon as stripped and blighted, that rebellious man should not enjoy her bright verdure and her accustomed fruits. These were destroyed by the catterpillar, the frosts, and locusts. Diseases and violence prevailed among men, and madness among animals, and fear fell upon the minds of the people. Measles, small-pox, camp-fever, and the Hessian fly; drafting, imprisonments, billetting of soldiers, and occupation of Meeting Houses for hospitals, came with the war. But the war ended after seven years; the Friends acquiesced in the change; made their friendly address to General Washington, as President of the United States, and received a kind response from him who always respected their conscientious convictions. Nature and Friends again assumed a happy aspect; but to the minds of Friends a dark cloud yet rested upon the nation, still threatening a Divine retribution, so long as the sons of Africa were kept in bondage, and the Indians suffered wrong by the encroachments of white men. The day of deliverance came at last for the slaves, not as Friends would have wished by peaceful means, yet by means permitted by Him to whom vengeance belongeth; and the liberated slaves, and yet extant Indians claim their aid in common with our paternal government.

In conclusion I would say that the efforts of our Society have not begun to soon. Many materials exist that are daily passing away among the descendants of old families that would illustrate history, and interest deeply our descendants in our most worthy ancestors. More of these exist in the custody of the Meetings of Friends and among their descendants than in any equal number of our citizens. Those belonging to the Meetings are not easily accessible to those not in membership; yet it is evident that Dr. Smith's History of Delaware county has been much enriched from that source; Dr. Michener's Early Retrospect of Quakerism is made up from that source; and Comly's Friends' Miscellany in twelve volumes, contains only matters that relate to that Religious Society.

THE PLEASURES

OF

NUMISMATIC SCIENCE.

A PAPER READ BEFORE THE NUMISMATIC AND ANTIQUARIAN SOCIETY
OF PHILADELPHIA, AT A STATED MEETING
HELD OCT. 4TH, 1866.

BY

HENRY PHILLIPS, JR.

" Et genus et formam, regina pecunia donat."—Hor. Ep. i. vi. 37.

PHILADELPHIA:
1867.

THE PLEASURES OF NUMISMATIC SCIENCE.

AMONG all branches of Archæology, there is none more interesting, none which will better repay the assiduity of the student than that to which we devote a portion of our associated efforts. I refer to the Science of Numismatics; a pursuit whose paramount importance in the study of antiquities is becoming every day more and more apparent and more thoroughly appreciated. It is an absolute science that has passed through the regular gradations of existence. In its earliest life facts were collected from which in later times theories were fabricated, and the superstructure of truth, freed from error and uncertainty, was finally raised upon its present solid foundation.

The value which Numismatics possesses as a powerful adjunct to Archæological researches, and the rewards of pleasure which it affords to its followers, are the topics upon which I propose to dilate, having chosen them from amidst all other subjects germane to our organization.

I do not, for one instant, suppose that the crude thoughts and fancies, which I, to-night, am about to submit to the judgment of the learned and accomplished gentlemen who compose our Society, will be found to contain any novelty, either in the choice or in the treatment of the subject. This short and imperfect essay has been prepared for the edification of those who are but newly joined to us in our Antiquarian pursuits; whose zeal and energies but require the right impetus to render them most useful members; whose knowledge of such matters may perhaps not be equal to their wishes.

With this apology, I must ask of the Society for my imperfect ideas, a lenient criticism and a favorable hearing; that they will not too harshly judge the deficiencies between the conception and the performance; that they will remember however great the zeal, how poor may be the powers of execution.

Coins and coinage betoken that the last steps have been taken by a community in its progress towards civilization. Rude indeed is the condition of those tribes whose daily wants are to be supplied by the barter of commodities; whilst necessarily, those nations must be of a polished mind whose life is surrounded by art and its varied refinements. And coins and coinage are the ultimate degrees to which artistic nurture arrives.

"The currency of a people is the index of the degree of civilization to which it has attained," and presents to us at one comprehensive view, better than mere force of words, the knowledge of its æsthetic perfection. " Documentary evidence may be altered in a thousand ways; inscriptions may be added and fabricated long after the period to which they apparently belong. Art is however *always* the expression of some contemporaneous idea, and conveys it unaltered to the latest times. No monarch, however absolute, can make the art of his time other than the expression of the feeling of that age; nor can he make it better than the advancement of his people at that time can afford. Art, is therefore, always an intelligible contemporary ; one which, when rightly read, cannot deceive, and tells its tale with a distinctness no writing can afford."* When, for example, we view one of the beautiful coins of Syracuse, we can feel and know how very much cultivated, educated and refined must have been the community among which they were wont to circulate ; and when we behold the coinage of China or Siam, we can perceive intuitively how far removed from thorough civilization, how degraded and barbarous must be the natives of such a country !

The pursuit of Art Beauty argues intelligence, and may find a just direction in the collection of coins. Beauty reveals herself to the accomplished Numismatist amid the manifold perfections of ancient excellence to which as yet Modern Art has not attained. We have striven for centuries after antique

* Ferguson's Nineveh and Persepolis.

models, without being able to invent a single improvement on those standard forms.

He who possesses a cabinet of coins, holds within a small compass an encyclopædia of the world's progress. He has there its history, its geography, ethnology, linguistics, chronology, natural history, architecture, and indeed there is scarcely any science relating to this mundane sphere and its inhabitants, which may not receive some accession of knowledge from a Numismatic collection thoroughly studied out and appreciated. "Many things," says Priestly, "have coins preserved to us, both in nature and art, which writers have passed unnoticed as being too familiar in the times in which they wrote, or have omitted, not being aware that they would ever engage the attention of future ages." Raphael, Rubens, Le Bruyn, and other celebrated painters, are said to have formed Numismatic collections in order to thoroughly study them; so exact and so delicate, so lofty in expression, so fine in relief, are the coinages of the ancient Greeks.

To enjoy to the full, the pleasures of our science, is the province and the privilege of the scholar. With no thought of success, with no such anticipations of exceeding gratification, can the unlettered or the sciolist hope to enter within the purlieus of this fascinating pursuit; all knowledge must bear its portion and contribute to this study, so productive of results. Those who value a coin by its price or by its rarity, unimpressed by the interest awakened by the piece itself, or uncharmed by the artistic excellence of its execution, are not *collectors ;* such are mere speculators, of which unfortunately there are already too many.

But those to whom an inanimate piece of metal recalls the days when it was a living currency, passing from hand to hand as our money does now, a representative of absolute value— those whom its sight transports back to the shadowy time in the far distant past, when *other human beings like ourselves,* in feelings and in sensations, aims, objects and actions, made the acquisition of such money their perpetual struggle, as we do now for "*the almighty dollar ;*" the possession of a store of such coins to constitute their wealth and happiness; those who can *realize* all these things, those so highly gifted by nature and by education, hold within themselves a source of pleasure of which they can never be deprived!

"To such they do not present themselves as mere unmeaning lists of names and things, but as voices of *men* who lived and died, centuries upon centuries past, and who expressed their feelings and their aspirations in those forms, we now gaze upon and try to understand, being face to face, as it were, with him who lived *two thousand years ago*,"* and saw these coins as they emanated fresh from officina of the mint, and examined the workmanship and read the inscriptions as we do *now!* What he saw and felt, it is our privilege to see and to feel, and all these things we may know if we will but give ourselves the trouble to study and to understand."

I open a cabinet of coins and in a moment I am in fairy land. I can transport myself back almost to the first eras of human life; I can at will raise before my mind a vision of the past, but as vivid and as ineffaceable as though it were of to-day.

The earliest gold coins known, the staters of the Greeks and the daries of the Persians, recall to us the dawn of the history of the Eastern world. To a period fully eight hundred years before our own era, may these coins with safety be alloted and disclose to our minds the fabled wealth of the Orient, and the internecine conflicts of the Greek Republics and States, and the early and close connections between Hellas and the Eastern world.

The singular silver coinage of Ægina, with the rude device of a turtle, emblematical of the island floating on the surface of the ocean, and bearing on the reverse the rude punch mark, so demonstrative of the first era of coinage, bring instantly to our recollection the busy trading marts of the Mediterranean once resonant with the hum of colonies sent out time after time from the overflow of the Phœnician hive.

I view a coin of Alexander, and thereon we may often trace

* Ferguson's Persepolis and Nineveh.

his successive conquests by the varying mint mark. Sometimes the conqueror's head appears under the disguise of Pallas; sometimes the horned head recalls the boasted descent
from Ammon. In the distant East the fame of this potent
monarch is even at the present time preserved, and his prowess
is still related as of Eskander Dulkârnein, "Alexander, the two
horned."

The magnificent coinage of the Ptolemy's, the descendants
of the lieutenant of Alexander, evoke instantly a vision of
Alexandria, the metropolis of ancient philosophy and learning,
the rival of Athens, the site of the world-renowned Library.
The mechanical execution and artistic taste of the coins themselves, is almost unsurpassable; the noble eagles found especially on the reverses of the large bronzes betoken the highest
grade of æsthetic refinement. We find on this series the history of an unbroken line of Egyptian monarchs, from its origin
in the Macedonian general through a varying descent of valor
and ability to its close in Cleopatra, whose face as represented
on her coins reveals none of that traditionary beauty which
captivated successively the rulers of the Roman Empire, and
for which, even at a matured age, Mark Antony infatuated, gave
up the whole world.

Athens claims a passing glance, and there we discover imperishably enshrined the attributes of Pallas Athenè, its tutelary goddess. While the Parthenon and the proud fanes which
once graced Hellas, have crumbled into dust long since scat-
tered to the four winds of heaven—this despised and rejected
witness bears mute, but unerring testimony, to the truths which
history has recorded of Greece.

With what contempt would that Athenian have been overwhelmed, if any such there had existed, while Attica was at
the height of its power, and at the summit of its glory, when
its arms were everywhere victorious, and its name respected
even by the *barbarians*, as these proud citizens were wont to
term all dwellers out of the charmed bounds of Hellas, while
all the arts and sciences and refinements of the known world
were centered around the Athenian capitol; with what wither-

ing scorn would such a prophet have been received had he
ventured to predict those events with which we are now so
thoroughly and so sadly familiar! "Two thousand years shall
scarce have passed away, and your cities, now so full of the
scenes of busy life, shall be howling wildernesses, heaps of dust
and ruins, inhabited but by the wild denizens of the mountain
and of the forest; your palaces, monuments and temples over-
thrown and crumbled away into nothingness and long forgotten ; your very existence and prowess made a matter of historic
doubt and research; and the most permanent attestation
that shall remain of your chiefest glories, of your arts and
refinements and cultivated tastes, shall be these pieces of metal
which you treat with such disdain; with which on one day you
free yourselves from the importunities of a beggar, and on the
next purchase for yourselves your food, your lodging, your
raiment; with which you gain admittance to the theatres, to
the stadia, to the baths; by which you acquire the necessaries
of every day life. . That upon these coins and upon these alone
shall depend much of your future fame. From that source
shall history be restored, the exploits of princes recorded, and
the buildings and images now so familiar to you, be brought
back from oblivion's dark shades to the light of knowledge!"

No madhouse could have been found wherein such a Cas-
sandra could have received a treatment sufficiently harsh, to
correspond to his apparently hideously disordered intellect.

And yet all the changes spoken of have came to pass, and
much knowledge of those ancient days, their manners, men and
customs, only remain to us in these forms. Fossils have been
aptly styled "The medals of Creation;" we may truthfully
reverse this saying, and designate coins as "the fossils of
humanity." A coin alone preserves to us the sole resemblance
of the theatre of Dionysos at Athens; "upon a coin alone is
preserved to us the palace at Verona of Theodoric (or Deittrich)
the Goth; a strange building with domes and minarets something like a Turkish mosque, standing seemingly upon the
arcades of some older building. Hence may Theodoric the

Goth be called the founder of Byzantine architecture in the Western world."*

As Pinkerton has well observed, "Triumphal arches, temples, fountains, aquaducts, cerci, theatres, hippodromes, palaces, basilicas, columns and obelisks, baths, seaports, pharoses and such like * * * * are often found in perfect preservation on medals and there only." "The great men of antiquity all pass in review before us, and the different countries of the then known world, are also delineated with great poetical imagery."†

> The medal, faithful to its charge of fame,
> Through climes and ages bears each form and name;
> In one short view, subjected to our eye,
> Gods, emperors, heroes, sages, beauties lie.
>
> POPE.

Coins alone tell the history of the Bactrian kings, the remotest of all the conquests of the great Alexander, and the narrative of their recovery and interpretation, is among the most interesting events of the present wonderful century. In the year 1808, a single coin found near the shores of the Caspian Sea, and preserved in the cabinet of a Russian prince, embraced within itself our whole knowledge of the kingdom of Bactria. Since then the British aggressions in the East have led to the discovery of many series of such pieces, and the most important results have ensued. "This recently discovered series is especially interesting," says Humphreys, " as having been the means of recovering many facts concerning the history of a portion of Asia, which, during a long period, was lost in obscurity; and also as being the means of restoring at the same time, a lost language. The inscriptions on some of the coins being bilingual, Greek on one side, and the Indian dialect of the region on the other."

And the very names of coins themselves may reveal and enlighten historic truth. "The GUINEA was so called because coined from gold brought from the *Guinea* coast. The BYZANT, a large gold coin of the value of £15 sterling, was struck at

* Kingsley's "Roman and Teuton."   † Pinkerton.

Byzantium. The DOLLAR, was originally the same as the German THALER, which took its name from the silver works in the *Thal,* a valley of Joachim. The FLORIN was struck at *Florence;* the MARK was a Venetian coin stamped with the winged lion of St. Mark. CUFIC coins, Arabic silver pieces, were struck at Cufa. The JANE, which is mentioned by Chaucer and Spencer, was a small coin of Genoa (*Janua*). The FRANC is *nummus francicus,* money of the Franks or of the French; and the Dutch GUILDER, may possibly take its name from *Gulderland.* * * * * A DUCAT is a coin issued by a *duke,* just as a SOVEREIGN is that issued by a *king.* A TESTER bore the image of the king's head, (*teste* or tête), and the PENNY *may perhaps* be in like manner the diminutive of the Celtic *Pen,* a head. The Welch word *ceiniog,* a penny, is analogously from *ceinn,* a head. A SHILLING or SKILLING, bore the device of a *schild or shield,* and a SCUDO, had a *scutum.*"*

I have digressed to show this phase of the value of Numismatics. Such a list could be almost indefinitely extended, and in the future I trust to be able to lay before the Society some additional and interesting information on the subject.

From the ponderous Roman æs, we can recall the rule of Servius Tullus, with his wise institutions; from the (so called) family coins and their traditionary legends, the free days of the Republic. The valor of Horatius Cocles, the treachery of Tarpeia, the dream of Scylla, the monetary implements of the Romans, the perpetual dictatorship of Cæsar, and the Ides of March, live on these coins forever. Imperishably shrined are the records of the events thus commemorated.

We can trace the rise and progress of the Roman Empire through its twelve vulturine centuries, with its mutability of rulers, and changes of civilization. We can see the loss of power from the senate and from the people, and its accretion to their one Supreme Master. We mark the weak mind of Caligula, and the surly visage of Nero; we can feel the gluttony of Vitellius, the dandyism of Otho, the harshness and

* Taylor's Names and Places.

severity of Galba, and the benignity of Titus, "Deliciæ humani generis;" we can note the beauty of Poppœa, and of Faustina.

Far down the long line, through good and bad, and worse and worst rulers, tyrants, usurpers, down to the founding of the Eastern Empire, extend these noble "pledges of history," bearing historical records of inestimable value ; the anniversary of the 1000th year of Rome's existence is found celebrated upon them, thus giving valuable data to the Chronologist.

With the Christian emperors, the type of the coinage changed; the symbols of the worship of Christ now appeared where gods and godesses and tutelary genii were wont to rule. But not on the coins of the first Christian emperor, strange as it may appear, are found these alterations. The only coin attributed to Constantine the Great, on which are found the emblems of his newly adopted religious faith, is considered by the most competent and experienced judges to be spurious. And the coins struck at his decease, represent his deification in the same style as was wont to be customary in the good old orthodox pagan times.

The sun of Roman civilization went down in blood; the pall of intellectual darkness was over the face of the earth. A glimmer of light soon manifested itself, and spread into a bright blaze as a beacon for the mind of man to follow. The dispersion of the knowledge which had been so long the exclusive property of the East, proved the sunrise of the intellect of Western Europe. Men of learning, driven by their barbarian conquerors from Constantinople, settled in France and Italy. The glorious eras of Medicean civilization have often been described; they have never been equalled since, in the generous rewards then extended to learning, and the assiduous care with which it was preserved and fostered. Culture of literature and the fine arts was diffused, and we now find the records of Numismatic Science. "Nobles and individuals began to vie with each other in discovering and preserving zealously these most interesting and intelligent relics of antiquity, although at first chiefly with the object of obtaining

10

portraits of those who had been most conspicuous in the world's past history, and soon learned treatises began to appear upon the subject. A Spaniard, Antonio Agostino, has the honor of publishing the first work upon this science, and which quickly was translated into many other languages. The great names of Strada, Lazius, Orsini, Occo and Goltz, are indelibly connected with the early advances of the science, and since their era, many hundreds of others have become illustrious in Numismatic history. Petrarca rendered himself no less conspicuous through his poetical talents than through his eager investigations of Roman history, literature and antiquities, and his earnest assiduity in the collection of coins. The donation of coins made by him to the Emperor Charles IV., is as well known as the patriotic advice with which the gift was accompanied.

Alphonso, King of Aragon, caused to be brought to him the ancient coins which were discovered in Italy, and carried them always in an ivory cabinet, confessing by their contemplation, his soul was incited to great deeds.

We could fill unlimited space to prove that at the revival of letters the science partook of the general enthusiasm, but these few examples may suffice to show how great a pleasure and a profit the most illustrious and learned derived from its pursuit.

Many were the uses to which the science was directed, and numerous were the errors into which it was distorted during several centuries; to write them would be but to indite a history of human progress, slow, overwhelmed with doubts, struggling with uncertainties, until at last, emerging from chaos, darkness and confusion, from the sloughs of falsity, it reached the highlands of truth where now so firmly is its seat established.

The very same century that witnessed the downfall and the extinction of the last vestiges of the old Roman Empire, the whilome mistress of the world, beheld the invention of Printing and the discovery of America! Singular impressions are conveyed to our minds by this wonderful collocation of facts. Old ideas and feelings were being obliterated; the world had ripened to receive a new phase of existence. Long were the preparations by which the Divinity had gradually smoothed the way for the change; arduous were the workings in the laboratory of nations; the time had now arrived, and we the fortunate dwellers in America are privileged to behold the newly discovered art, here in the newly discovered country, carried to that point of perfection from whence the greatest benefit shall issue to mankind.

Nor yet alone with the coinage of the *ancient* world need our researches cease. The Numismatics of the middle ages present an interesting study, revealing the existence and prominence of many potentates and states, now blotted out from the view of the world or fallen upon evil times. Time will not permit that I should enlarge upon this subject, nor yet upon that of modern coinage. We have thus gone over the prominent features in the history of the inhabited globe, and a well furnished cabinet can give rise to many more thorough and deep reflections.

Numerous and great are the pleasures of our pursuit. We hold the true secrets of magic. No enchantments do we need, no wand, no fumigations, no circles of grinning skulls! We possess *another* philosophy, one more intellectual, one more potent! We take into our hands an inanimate piece of metal. What a wonder! We utter no mighty words, but the curtain of time which covers the yawning, unfathomable abyss of oblivion, has rolled back twenty centuries for our gratification! Two thousand years have stood still; we are conscious of a double existence, one in the present and one in the past; the mind expands into the most distant eras. The hand of time has gone backwards two thousand markings on the dial of eternity. Eternity itself is no more!

A cyclopean wall, an aged tree, a huge rock, objects possessing stability, to the ancients appeared as the only things endowed with immortality and capable of perpetuating their remembrance. And yet where are they now?

The story of Washington Irving and the Spanish monk, that mournful tale of human weakness, is here forcibly exemplified. The actors in life's drama have all departed to their long homes, leaving but these slight tokens of their having ever existed.

The animate objects are gone; the inanimate alone remain FOREVER!

A

HISTORICAL SKETCH

OF THE

NATIONAL MEDALS

ISSUED PURSUANT TO

RESOLUTION OF CONGRESS, 1776-1815.

A PAPER READ BEFORE

"𝔗𝔥𝔢 𝔑𝔲𝔪𝔦𝔰𝔪𝔞𝔱𝔦𝔠 𝔞𝔫𝔡 𝔄𝔫𝔱𝔦𝔮𝔲𝔞𝔯𝔦𝔞𝔫 𝔖𝔬𝔠𝔦𝔢𝔱𝔶 𝔬𝔣 𝔓𝔥𝔦𝔩𝔞𝔡𝔢𝔩𝔭𝔥𝔦𝔞,"

THURSDAY EVENINGS, NOVEMBER 1 AND 15, 1866,

BY

CHARLES H. HART,

CORRESPONDING SECRETARY.

PHILADELPHIA:
1867.

NATIONAL MEDALS.

I PROPOSE to read before the Society this evening, a brief memoir of the National Medals awarded by Congress during the Revolutionary War, the *quasi* French War, and the War of 1812. This idea suggested itself to me, by reading in the *Evening Bulletin* last week, an article copied from the New York *Sun*, on this same subject; but this article was so full of blunders and gross and ridiculous errors, that it was calculated more to mislead than to direct any one in the pursuit of their investigations. They number forty-one.

The medals of the Revolution were all struck in France, and at the time they were issued, the French Government presented a series in silver to General Washington, which series it is said, after his decease, were offered for sale and purchased by Daniel Webster? So highly esteemed were these records of the Revolution, that about the year 1791, an enterprising Jew in London, by the name of Hyams, who had seen them, cut at his own expense dies of several, and executed copies in copper, which were sold as genuine. The copper medals of Washington, Howard and William Washington, had their origin in this forgery.

By a resolution of Congress, March 25, 1776, the first National Medal was presented to General Washington, on the occasion of the evacuation of Boston by the British troops in that year. Also a vote of thanks was passed to him, and the officers and soldiers under his command, for their wise and spirited conduct in the seige and acquisition of the city. The size of this medal according to the scale adopted by this Society would be 42, and bears on the

Obverse. Undraped bust of Washington facing to the right. *Legend.* GEORGIO WASHINGTON SVPREMO DVCI EXERCITVVM ADSERTORI LIBERTATIS. Beneath is inscribed, COMITIA AMERI-

CANA. The name of the engraver, *Du Vivier, Paris, F.*, appears beneath the bust.

Reverse. In the background appears the city of Boston which the British troops are evacuating and retiring to their shipping. To the right are the American intrenchments, with the troops drawn up in front ready to march into the city. In the foreground on Dorchester Heights, is Washington and his staff mounted; on the ground are cannon and cannon balls. *Legend.* HOSTIBUS PRIMO FUGATIS. *Exergue.* BOSTONIUM RECUPERATUM XVII MARTII MDCCLXXVI.

The line of ownership of this most interesting memorial of the Father of our Country, I have been unable to trace, only that about two years since there appeared in the columns of the *Evening Bulletin*, the following paragraph: "*A Precious Relic.*—The only gold medal ever voted by Congress to General Washington is for sale, its owner, who has lost by the war everything else that is valuable, being compelled to part with it. It was given in honor of the evacuation of Boston by the British. On the obverse is a fine medallion profile of Washington, and on the reverse he and his staff are grouped on Bunker's Hill, while the British fleet is seen moving down the bay. It contains $180 worth of gold. It is in perfect preservation, having been guarded by its owner with the most religious care. Five thousand dollars have been offered for it; but to the Government or to a Historical Society, it would be worth much more. We shall be glad to give further information concerning it to parties that may desire it." I made no inquiries about it at the time, and now all recollection of it has been lost.

The next medal presented by Congress was to General Wayne, familiarly known as "Mad Anthony," for his famous attack and capture of Stony Point on the 15th of July, 1779. By the journals of Congress it appears that the attack was ordered by General Washington on the 10th of July, and on the morning of the 15th Wayne issued his orders, and on the night of the same day the attack was successfully made. Eleven days afterwards, or on the 26th, Congress passed a vote

141

of thanks to General Wayne, and the officers and soldiers under
his command, particularly mentioning Colonel De Fleury and
Major Stewart who led the attacking columns, and Lieutenants
Gibbons and Knox, who, under a severe fire, destroyed the
double row of *abatis*. Gibbons and Knox were promoted, and
a gold medal was ordered to be presented to General Wayne,
and silver ones to Colonel De Fleury and Major Stewart.
The
Obverse of the Wayne medal bears an Indian queen, holding
in her left hand a mural crown towards General Wayne, while
with her right she is presenting him with a wreath of laurel.
General Wayne holds his chapeau in his left hand, and is
receiving the wreath with his right. At the feet of the queen
an alligator is stretched out, resting upon which is a shield
bearing the arms of the United States, and from under her feet
appears a bow. *Legend.* ANTONIO WAYNE DUCI EXERCITUS.
Exergue. COMITIA AMERICANA. *Gatteaux.*
Reverse. A double turreted fort upon an eminence, with
troops advancing in front and rear up the hill in Indian file to
storm it. Another party is being led, with charged bayonets,
over *abatis* in the foreground in pursuit of a retreating enemy.
Ships are in sight upon the river, and troops are advancing
along the shore. *Legend.* STONY POINT EXPUGNATUM. *Exergue.* XV JUL., MDCCLXXIX. *Gatteaux.* It is size 34.
The size of the De Fleury medal is 29, and has for its
Obverse. A soldier helmeted standing among the ruins of a
fort trampling upon a flag with his right foot, the staff of which
he holds in his left hand. In his right hand, which is extended,
he carries a naked sword. *Legend.* VIRTUTIS ET AUDACIÆ
MONUM. ET PRÆMIUM. *Exergue.* D. DE FLEURY EQUITI GALLO
PRIMO SUPER MUROS RESP. AMERIC. D. D. *Du Vivier, S.*
Reverse. A fort with two turrets and a flag flying upon a
hill overlooking the river below, upon which vessels are visible.
At the left base of the hill are two water batteries, one of which
is being discharged. *Legend.* AGGERES PALUDES HOSTES VICTI.
Exergue. STONY-PT. EXPUGN. XV JUL., MDCCLXXIX.

142

The third medal struck under the resolution of July 26, 1779, was for Major John Stewart.

Obverse. America personified in an Indian queen, is presenting a palm branch to Major Stewart; a quiver hangs at her back; her bow and an alligator at her feet; with her left hand she sustains a shield resting upon the ground and bearing the American arms. *Legend.* JOANNI STEWART COHORTIS PRÆ-FECTO. *Exergue.* COMITIA AMERICANA. *Gatteaux.*

Reverse, very much like the reverse of the Wayne medal, with the exception that the leader of the second party is the most prominent figure. *Legend.* STONY POINT OPPUGNATUM. *Exergue.* XV JUL., MDCCLXXIX. *Gatteaux.* Size 34.

The fifth medal was a gold one presented to Major Henry Lee, nick-named Light Horse Harry, by resolution of Congress passed September 24, 1779, "for the remarkable prudence, address and bravery displayed by him in his attack upon a body of British troops and the fort at Paulus Hook," now Jersey City, "on the 19th of August, 1779."

Obverse. Profile bust of Major Lee in regimentals. *Legend.* HENRICO LEE LEGIONIS EQUIT. PRÆFECTO. *Exergue.* COMITIA AMERICANA.

Reverse. A wreath of oak and olive leaves. *Legend.* NON OBSTANTIB. FLUMINIBUS, VALLIS, ASTUTIA ET VIRTUTE BELLICA, PARVA MANU HOSTE VICIT VICTOSQ. ARMIS HUMANITATE DIVINXIT. IN MEM. PUGN. AD PAULUS HOOK. DIE XIX AUG., 1779. Size 36.

By resolution of Congress of November 4, 1779, a gold medal was ordered to be struck and presented to General Gates, in commemoration of the surrender of Lieutenant-General Burgoyne and his army at Saratoga, October, 1777. This is not the place nor have I the desire, to enter into an argument on the subject, whether General Gates was exactly the proper officer to receive a medal commemorating this important event in our Revolutionary history. *Sufficit* to say that all close students of our country's annals about this time, will well know the just claims of General Philip Schuyler to that opening cloud in the dark days of our first struggle for freedom.

Obverse. Head of General Gates in profile. *Legend.* HORA-TIO GATES DUCI STRENUO. *Exergue.* COMITIA AMERICANA. Name of the engraver *N. Gatteaux*, below the bust.

Reverse. General Burgoyne, in front of his troops who are grounding their arms and laying down their colors, is represented in the act of surrendering his sword to General Gates, at the head of the American line with their arms shouldered and their colors advanced. To the side of the commanders are a drum and colors. *Legend.* SALUS REGIONUM SEPTENTRIONAL. *Exergue.* HOSTE AD SARATOGAM IN DEDITION. ACCEPTO DIE XVII. OCT., MDCCLXXVII. Size 34.

By a vote of Congress 3d of November, 1780, " a silver medal or shield was ordered to be struck and presented to John Paulding," David Williams and Isaac Van Wart, who intercepted Major John Andre, in the character of a spy, and notwithstanding the large bribes offered them for his release, nobly disdaining to sacrifice their country for the sake of gold, secured and conveyed him to the commanding officer of the district, whereby the conspiracy of Benedict Arnold was brought to light, the insidious designs of the enemy baffled, and the United States rescued from impending danger." A pension of two hundred dollars annually during life was also bestowed on each of them. These medals were not struck but chased.

Obverse. A raised shield surrounded by branches of laurel and palm. *Legend.* FIDELITY.

Reverse. A wreath formed of palm branches enclosing a blank for the insertion of the name of the recipient. *Legend.* VINCIT AMOR PATRIÆ. Size 26 by 34.

On the 17th of January, 1781, was fought the celebrated battle of the Cowpens, in which eighty cavalry and two hundred and thirty-seven infantry of the United States, and five hundred and fifty-three Southern militia, obtained a complete victory over a select and well appointed detachment of more than eleven hundred British regulars, commanded by Lieutenant-Colonel Bannister Tarlton. On the following 9th of March, Congress resolved to present to General Daniel Morgan a gold medal, and to Colonels John Egar Howard and William Augustine Washington, silver ones, in honor of this victory, in which they all participated.

The medal to Morgan has for the

Obverse. An Indian queen with a quiver on her back, in the act of crowning an officer with a laurel wreath ; his hand resting on his sword ; a cannon lying on the ground with an American shield resting against it ; various military weapons and implements in the background. *Legend.* DANIELI MORGAN DUCI EXERCITUS. *Exergue.* COMITIA AMERICANA. *Dupre, F.*

Reverse. A mounted officer leading his troops who carry the American colors, in pursuit of a retreating enemy bearing the British flag. In the background a general engagement is taking place, and in front a personal combat between an unhorsed dragoon and a foot soldier. *Legend.* VICTORIA LIBERTATIS VINDEX. *Exergue.* FVGATIS CAPTIS AUT CAESIS AD COWPENS HOSTIBVS. XVII JAN., MDCCLXXXI. *Dupre inv. et f.* Size 36.

The medal to Colonel Howard is

Obverse. A mounted officer pursuing and about to strike down with his uplifted sword a retreating foot soldier bearing a stand of colors. Between them victory is descending holding in her right hand a wreath of laurel over the officer's head, and in her left a palm branch. *Legend.* JOH. EGAR. HOWARD LEGIONIS PEDITUM PRÆFECTO. *Exergue.* COMITIA AMERICANA. *Duviv.*

Reverse. A laurel wreath. *Legend.* QUOD IN NUTANTEM HOSTIUM ACIEM SUBITO IRRUENS PRÆCLARUM BELLICÆ VIRTUTIS SPECIMEN DEDIT IN PUGNA AD COWPENS. XVII JAN., MDCCLXXXI. Size 30.

The last one of the Cowpen medals has

Obverse. An officer mounted at the head of a body of cavalry, charging flying troops ; Victory holding a laurel crown in her right hand and a palm branch in her left, hovers over the heads of the pursuing party. *Legend.* GULIELMO WASHINGTON LEGIONIS EQUIT. PRÆFECTO. *Exergue.* COMITIA AMERICANA. *Duv.* (Name of the engraver, Duvivier ?)

Reverse. A laurel wreath. *Legend.* QUOD PARVA MILITUM MANU STRENUE PROSECUTUS HOSTES VIRTUTIS INGENITÆ PRÆ-

CLARUM SPECIMEN DEDIT IN PUGNA AD COWPENS. XVII JAN.,
MDCCLXXXI. Size 28.

The last military medal presented during the Revolution,
was a gold one to General Nathaniel Greene, according to Act
of Congress, passed October 29, 1781, for his gallant conduct
at the battle of Eutaw Springs, South Carolina, September 8,
1781.

Obverse. Profile head of General Greene in uniform. *Legend.*
NATHANIELI GREEN EGREGIO DUCI. COMITIA AMERICANA.

Reverse. Victory, bearing in her left hand a palm branch
and holding in her upraised right a wreath of laurel, is in the
act of alighting upon the earth stepping on a broken shield,
beneath and about which another shield, broken arms, a laurel
branch and colors are lying. *Dupre.* *Legend.* SALUS REGIO-
NUM AUSTRALIUM. *Exergue.* HOSTIBUS AD EUTAW DEBELLATIS
DIE VIII. SEPT., MDCCLXXXI. Size 36.

Here ends the series of medals awarded to officers of the
army for meritorious actions during that long struggle, which
finally ended with the bonds being broken forever, which bound
us to our mother country ; and indeed but one more remains of
any kind, that to Captain John Paul Jones, for his capture of
the Serapis of 44 guns, commanded by Captain Pearson, by
the Bon Homme Richard of 40 guns, on the 23d of September,
1779, after a very severe engagement by moonlight, of four
hours duration, in which Jones lost his ship and 132 men killed
and wounded. On receiving the intelligence of this brave action,
Congress passed resolutions complimenting its hero, and six
years later, on October 16, 1787, came to the following :

Resolved. That the Congress entertain a high sense of the
distinguished bravery and military conduct of John Paul
Jones, Esq., Captain in the Navy of the United States, and
particularly in his victory over the British frigate Serapis,
on the coast of England, which was attended with circumstances
so brilliant as to excite general applause and admiration.

Resolved. That a *gold medal* be struck and presented to the
Chevalier Paul Jones, in commemoration of the valor and bril-

liant services of that officer; and that the Hon. Mr. Jefferson, Minister Plenipotentiary of the United States at the court of Versailles, have the same executed in France with proper devices.

The medal above alluded to is

Obverse. Bust of Captain Jones. *Legend.* JOANNI PAVLO JONES CLASSIS PRÆFECTO. *Exergue.* COMITIA AMERICANA.

Reverse. A representation of the engagement between the Bon Homme Richard and the Serapis, which are grappled yard-arm and yard-arm; the latter vessel is severely battered in the sides. The Countess of Scarborough, of 22 guns, the consort of the Serapis, is lying across her bows. Sailors are in the water clinging to floating spars. *Legend.* HOSTIVM NAVIBVS CAPTIS AVT FVGATIS. *Exergue.* AD ORAM SCOTIAE XXIII. SEPT., MDCCLXXVIIII. *Dupre, F.* Size 35.

Scarcely had this country settled down into the channels of peace, when once more it was called upon to assert its rights, and this time against a former ally—France. By the French marine ordinance of 26th July, 1778, a passport fully showing the national character of the bearer, is ranked among the proofs of neutrality which cannot be dispensed with in a prize court. In April, 1793, France being then engaged in a maritime war which might give application to the ordinance of 1778, the French minister for foreign affairs announced to Governeur Morris, then representing the United States, that M. Genét had been instructed to require of this government, that all American vessels should be "furnished with a passport agreeable to the model annexed to the treaty of 1778," so as "to prevent all difficulty that might arise in that respect."

In consequence probably of this representation, Mr. Jefferson arranged the form of a passport in accordance with the treaty, and an executive circular, dated 15th August, 1793, directed every American vessel to be provided with it before leaving this country. Still vessels claiming to be American were frequently found without the passport, and France complained that the American flag was thus permitted to be a cover for gross evasions of the belligerent rights. In the year 1796, these complaints assumed a sterner form, and were accompanied by a declaration that vessels without a passport would incur the penalty of condemnation as belligerents. From this time France continued to maintain the same doctrine, and to capture and condemn all American vessels that were found on the high seas without the treaty passport. The war of reprisals followed in 1798, and continued till the convention of 1800.

It was for an action which occurred in this last mentioned war, commonly called the *quasi* French war, that Congress awarded by resolution of the 24th of March, 1800, a gold medal to Captain Thomas Truxtun, as gallant an officer as ever walked the quarter-deck, for the action between the American frigate Constellation of 38 guns, commanded by Captain Truxtun, and the French frigate La Vengeance of 54 guns off Gaudaloupe, on the 1st of February, 1800. The description of the medal is

Obverse. Head of Captain Truxtun. *Legend.* PATRIAE PATRES FILIO DIGNO. THOMAS TRUXTUN.

Reverse. An engagement between two ships of war; both vessels are much shattered and their rigging much cut. *Legend.* THE UNITED STATES FRIGATE CONSTELLATION, OF THIRTY-EIGHT GUNS, PURSUES, ATTACKS, AND VANQUISHES THE FRENCH SHIP LA VENGEANCE, OF FIFTY-FOUR GUNS, 1ST OF FEB., 1800. *Exergue.* BY VOTE OF CONGRESS TO THOMAS TRUXTUN. 24 MAR., 1800. Size 35.

But a short time elapsed ere the United States was again forced to appeal to arms, and fitted out a squadron against the Algerian pirates on the coast of Barbary. This expedition was brought to a close by the memorable bombardment of Tripoli, on the 3d of August, 1804, an event well known to all readers of history. The fleet was commanded by Commodore Edward Preble, to whom Congress presented a gold medal by vote of March 3, 1805, for his brilliant victory and signal ability in negotiating a treaty of commerce and amity between his own government and that of the Bey of Tunis and Tripoli.

Obverse. Bust of Commodore Preble. *Legend.* EDWARDO PREBLE DUCI STRENUO. *Exergue.* COMITIA AMÉRICANA.

Reverse. The American fleet bombarding the town and forts of Tripoli. *Legend.* VINDICI COMMERCII AMERICANI. *Exergue.* ANTE TRIPOLI, MDCCCIV. Size 40.

We now reach the period in our country's history which revealed her as one of the leading maritime powers of the globe. The war of 1812, or second war of American Independence, was mainly caused by the claims of Great Britain to the right of search in times of peace, and the impressment of seamen into their navy from foreign merchantmen, under the pretended theory of non-recognition of the right of expatriation.

The earliest battle of importance in this war, the one which may be said to have fairly opened the ball, was that fought on the 19th of August, 1812, between the United States frigate Constitution, 44 guns, commanded by Isaac Hull, of Philadelphia, and H. B. M. frigate Guerriere, 50 guns, Captain Dacres, in which the latter vessel was captured after an action of thirty minutes, with the loss of seventy-seven men killed and wounded. Congress, on the 29th of January, 1813, passed a resolution presenting to Captain Hull for this victory a gold medal, and to each of the commissioned officers silver ones. Also the same to Captains Jacob Jones and Stephen Decatur, and their commissioned officers, the former for his capture of the English sloop-of-war Frolic, on the 20th of October, and the latter for taking the British frigate Macedonian, 50 guns, by the United States frigate United States, 44 guns, on the 25th of the same month and year.

These medals are Hull's.

Obverse. Bust of Captain Hull. *Legend.* PERITOS ARTE SUPERAT JUL., MDCCCXII AUG. CERTAMINE FORTES. *Exergue.* ISAACUS HULL.

Reverse. The battle between the Constitution and the Guerriere, is represented in that particular and interesting stage, when the boarders from the Guerriere were repulsed, and a raking fire from the Constitution had cut away the main and foremasts of the Guerriere, which are falling, leaving the American ship little injured. *Legend.* HORAE MOMENTO VICTORIA. *Exergue.* INTER CONST. NAV. AMER. ET GUER. ANGL. Size 40.

Jones'.

Obverse. Head of Captain Jones. *Legend.* IACOBUS JONES VIRTUS IN ARDUA TENDIT. *Furst, F.*

Reverse. Two ships closely engaged, the bowsprit of the Frolic has run between the main and mizzenmasts of the Wasp, and men are just in the act of boarding her from the bow of the Wasp ; the latter ship has her maintopmast shot away. *Legend.* VICTORIAM HOSTI MAJORI CELERRIME RAPUIT. *Exergue.* INTER WASP NAV. AMERI. ET FROLIC NAV., ANG. DIE XVIII, OCT., MDCCCXII. *Furst, F.* Size 40.

Decatur's.

Observe. Bust of Commodore Decatur. *Legend.* STEPHANUS DECATUR NAVARCHUS PUGNIS. *Exergue.* PLURIBUS, VICTOR. *Furst, F.*

Reverse. The engagement of the two frigates Macedonia and United States. The topmasts of the former are shot away, while the latter has but a few shots through her sails. *Legend.* OCCIDIT SIGNUM HOSTILE SIDERA SURGUNT. *Exergue.* INTER STA. UNI. NAV. AMERI. ET MACEDO. NAV. ANG. DIE XXV, OCTOBRIS, MDCCCXII. *Furst, F.* Size 40.

The next medal which comes under our notice, was given to one of our own citizens, of whom we have a just right to be proud, and I doubt not but some of the gentlemen before me may well remember him. I refer to Commodore William Bainbridge, whose respected widow, the mother-in-law of our gallant fellow-townsman, Captain Henry K. Hoff, still lives among us. It was awarded by resolve of Congress approved March 3, 1813, together with fifty thousand dollars to Captain Bainbridge, for his capture of the British frigate Java, 50 guns, after a desperate encounter lasting one hour and fifty-five minutes, by the United States frigate Constitution, 44 guns, a vessel better known to the present generation by its suitable *sobriquet* of "Old Ironsides."

11

Obverse. Bust of Captain Bainbridge. *Legend.* GULIELMUS BAINBRIDGE PATRIA VICTISQUE LAUDATUS. *Furst, F.*

Reverse. The Java is represented with all her masts shot away, only the three stumps remaining above deck. The Constitution on the other hand has but a few rents in her sails. *Legend.* PUGNANDO. *Exergue.* INTER CONST. NAV. AMERI. ET JAV. NAV. ANGL. DIE XXIX DECEM., MDCCCXII. *Furst, F.* Size 40.

This medal was of gold, and silver ones were presented to the commissioned officers serving under him on this occasion.

January 6, 1814, resolutions were passed by Congress awarding gold medals, to the nearest male relative of Lieutenant William Burrows, for the action between the British sloop-of-war Boxer and the American brig Enterprise, in which Lieutenant Burrows, commanding the Enterprise, was killed; to Lieutenant Edward R. McCall, of South Carolina, second in command during the engagement; to Commodore Oliver Hazard Perry, for his celebrated victory obtained upon Lake Erie, September 10, 1813, and to Captain Jesse Duncan Elliott, second in command under Perry; also silver ones to the other commissioned officers who participated in these conflicts.

The Burrows medal has for the

Obverse. An urn upon a tomb, surrounded by various military emblems, and a wreath hanging from a trident. The pedestal bears the name W. Burrows. *Legend.* VICTORIAM TIBI CLARAM PATRIÆ MÆSTAM.

Reverse. A view of the action between the Enterprise and Boxer, in sight of the coast. The Boxer has her maintopmast shot away. *Legend.* VIVERE SAT VINCERE. *Exergue.* INTER ENTERPRISE NAV. AMERI. ET BOXER NAV. BRIT. DIE IV SEPT., MDCCCXIII. *Furst, F.* Size 40.

The medal to Lieutenant McCall is

Obverse. Bust of Lieutenant McCall. *Legend.* EDWARD R. MCCALL, NAVIS ENTERPRISE PRÆFECTUS. *Exergue.* SIC ITUR AD ASTRA. *Furst, F.*

Reverse. Same as the last. Size 40.

Of the Lake Erie medals, the one to Perry has, as follows: *Obverse.* Bust of Commodore Perry. *Legend.* OLIVERUS H. PERRY, PRINCEPS-STAGNO ERINSE. *Exergue.* CLASSIM TO-TAM CONTUDIT. *Furst, F.*

Reverse. The American and British fleet closely engaged. *Legend.* VIAM INVENIT VIRTUS AUT FACIT. *Exergue.* INTER CLASS. AMERI. ET BRIT. DIE X, SEPT., MDCCCXIII. *Furst, F.* Size 40.

The one to Elliott.

Observe. Bust of Captain Elliott. *Legend.* JESSE D. ELLIOTT. NIL ACTUM REPUTANS SI QUID. *Exergue.* SUPERESSET AGEN-DUM. *Furst, F.*

Reverse. Same as last. Size 40.

"Don't give up the ship," as is well known, were the last words spoken by Captain James Lawrence aboard the Chesa-peake, when he was mortally wounded in the action with the Shannon, June 1, 1813, and which has since become the motto of the American navy. Two months before this memo-rable order was given, Captain Lawrence captured the English brig Peacock, 22 guns, by the United States war-sloop Hornet, 18 guns, for which service Congress by resolution of January 11, 1814, ordered a gold medal to be struck and presented to his nearest male relative.

Obverse. Head of Captain Lawrence. *Legend.* JAC. LAW-RENCE. DULCE ET DECORUM EST PRO PATRIA MORI. *Furst, F.*

Reverse. The Peacock with her mizzenmast gone is in the act of sinking bow foremost; a boat from her adversary is being rowed towards her. *Legend.* MANSUETUD. MAJ. QUAM VIC-TORIA. *Exergue.* INTER HORNET, NAV. AMERI. ET PEACOCK, NAV. ANG. DIE XXIV., FEB., MDCCCXIII. *Furst, F.* Size 40.

The commissioned officers of the Hornet received silver medals.

The second decisive naval victory which was gained on one of our great inland seas during this war, was that on the 11th of September, 1814, when Commodore Thomas Macdonough, with a fleet composed of four vessels and ten galleys carrying 86 guns, obtained a brilliant triumph over the British fleet of four vessels and thirteen galleys mounting 95 guns, on Lake Cham-plain. Gold medals were awarded to Captains Macdonough and Henley, and to Lieutenant Cassin, commorative of this victory, by resolution of Congress approved October 20, 1814.

Commodore Macdonough's medal has on the

Obverse. Bust of Captain Macdonough. *Legend.* THO. MAC-DONOUGH. STAGNO CHAMPLAIN CLAS. REG. BRIT. *Exergue.* SU-PERAVIT. *Furst, F.*

Reverse. Represents the engagement between the American and British fleets; several boats rowed by sailors are upon the lake; to the right Plattsburg is seen in flames. *Legend.* UNO LATERE PERCUSSO. ALTERUM IMPAVIDE VERTIT. *Exergue.* INTER CLASS. AMERI. ET BRIT. DIE XI, SEPT., MDCCCXIIII. *Furst, F.* Size 40.

Captain Henley's.

Obverse. Bust of Captain Henley. *Legend.* ROB. HENLEY EAGLE PRÆFECT. PALMA VIRTU. PER ÆTERNIT. FLOREBIT.

Reverse. Same as Macdonough's. Size 40.

Lieutenant Cassin's.

Obverse. Bust of Lieutenant Cassin. *Legend.* STEP. CASSIN, TICONDEROGA PRÆFECT. QUÆ REGIO IN TERRIS NOS. *Exergue.* NON PLENA LAB. *Furst, F.*

Reverse. Like the two last. Size 40.

Silver medals were awarded also to the commissioned officers of the American fleet, to the officers of the army serving in it during the contest, and to the nearest male relatives of Lieutenants Gamble and Stansbury, killed in the action.

The day succeeding the one on which were approved the resolutions presenting the three Champlain medals, Congress was again called upon to show its appreciation of native valor by ordering to be presented a gold medal to Captain Lewis Warrington, of Virginia, in honor of his victory over the Engligh brig-of-war Epervier, on the 29th of April, 1814.

Obverse. Bust of Captain Warrington. *Legend.* LUDOVICUS WARRINGTON, DUX NAVALIS AMERI. *Furst, F.*

Reverse. The engagement between the two vessels, the Epervier has her guns silenced and her topmasts shot away. *Legend.* PRO PATRIA PARATUS AUT VINCERE AUT MORI. *Exergue.* INTER PEACOCK NAV. AMERI. ET EPERVIE. NAV. ANG. DIE XXIX, MAR., MDCCCXIV. *Furst, F.* Size 40.

The date on the medal is undoubtedly an error by the die sinker, as the action did not take place until one month later, according to Captain Warrington's official letter to the Navy Department dated, "At sea April 29, 1814," and commencing, "We have this morning captured, after an action of forty-two minutes, his Majesty's brig Epervier * * * * &c."

For the capture, on the 28th of June, 1814, after an action of twenty-eight minutes duration, by the United States sloop-of war Wasp, of the British ship Reindeer, Captain Manners, a gold medal was awarded by resolution of Congress, dated November 3, 1814, to Captain Johnston Blakeley, who commanded the Wasp.

Obverse. Head of Captain Blakeley. *Legend.* JOHNSTON BLAKELEY, REIP. FÆD. AM. NAV. WASP DUX. *Furst, F.*

Reverse. A view of the engagement between the two vessels. The Reindeer's guns are silenced, and her colors pulled down in token of surrender. *Legend.* EHEU! BIS VICTOR PATRIA TUA TE LUGET PLAUDITQ. *Exergue.* INTER WASP NAV. AMERI. ET REINDEER NAV. ANG. DIE XXVIII JUNIUS MDCCCXIV. *Furst, F.* Size 40.

After the capture of the Reindeer, Captain Blakeley continued his cruise, and subsequently took the British sloop-of-war Avon, 20 guns, and brig Atalanta, the last on the 23d of September, 1814. On the 4th of the following October, the Wasp was spoken in latitude 18° 35′ N., longitude 30° 10′ W., from which time to this nothing has ever been heard of her. It is to this sad fate of Captain Blakeley that reference is made in the legend on the reverse of the foregoing medal.

We must now leave our naval patriots to return once more to our heroes on the land, whose engagements during the War of 1812–15, though not so brilliant and fortunate as their brethren of the sea, tended in a large degree to the successful termination of that series of conflicts which spread over the intervening time between the two last mentioned years.

On November 3, 1814, Congress passed a general resolution presenting gold medals to Generals Winfield Scott, Edmund Pendleton Gaines, Peter B. Porter, Jacob Brown,

James Miller, Eleazer W. Ripley and Alexander Macomb, in testimony of the high sense and appreciation entertained by that body, for their destinguished and meritorious services at the battles of Chippewa, Niagara, Erie and Plattsburg.

General Scott's for the battles of Chippewa and Niagara, has for the

Obverse. Bust of General Scott. *Legend*. MAJOR-GENERAL WINFIELD SCOTT. *Furst, F.*

Reverse. A snake entwined by a wreath of laurel and palm. *Legend*. RESOLUTION OF CONGRESS, NOVEMBER 3, 1814. BATTLES OF CHIPPEWA, JULY 5, 1814: NIAGARA, JULY 25, 1814. *Furst. F.* Size 40.

General Gaines', for his gallant defence of Fort Erie on the occasion of its attack by the British forces under General Drummond, on the 15th of August, 1814, has on the

Obverse. Head of General Gaines. *Legend*. MAJOR-GENERAL EDMUND P. GAINES. *Furst, F.*

Reverse. Victory standing upon a shield under which are a sword, musket, halberd and balls, and holding a palm branch in her left hand, is in the act of placing with her right hand a laurel crown upon the cascabel of a cannon, which is fixed upright in the ground with a scroll running round it, bearing the inscription " ERIE." Against one trunion rests a stand of British colors, and from the other is suspended a broadsword. On the ground to the right are a howitzer, helmet, and balls, trophies of victory, while behind the cannon is a helmet. *Legend*. RESOLUTION OF CONGRESS, NOVEMBER 3, 1814. *Exergue*. BATTLE OF ERIE, AUGUST 15, 1814. *Furst, F.* Size 40.

General Porter's, commemorative of all three battles, has for its

Obverse. Bust of General Porter. *Legend*. MAJOR-GENERAL PETER B. PORTER. *Furst, F.*

Reverse. Victory standing, bears in her right hand a laurel wreath and palm branch, and in her left she holds out three flags, inscribed severally, CHIPPEWA, NIAGARA, ERIE; the Muse of History, seated before her, is recording the victories at these places. *Legend.* RESOLUTION OF CONGRESS, NOV. 3, 1814. *Exergue.* BATTLES OF CHIPPEWA, JULY 5, 1814; NIAGARA, JULY 25, 1814; ERIE, SEPT. 17, 1814. *Furst, F.* Size 40.

It may be well to account for the disparity in dates between the Gaines and Porter medals of the battle of Erie, by stating that there were a series of conflicts between the two forces, commencing about the 4th of August and extending until the 17th of September, when the enemy were completely routed by the American forces under General Jacob Brown. On the 15th of August, the enemy were first repulsed at Fort Erie, by General Gaines.

General Brown's for the same.

Obverse. Head of General Brown. *Legend.* MAJOR-GENERAL JACOB BROWN. *Furst, F.*

Reverse. The Roman fasces indicative of the union and strength of the States, surrounded upon both sides by stands of British colors, swords, muskets, and other military emblems, and from the top hangs a wreath of laurel, from which are suspended three tablets, bearing the inscription, NIAGARA, ERIE. CHIPPEWA; and in front at its base the American eagle is standing upon the British flag. *Legend.* RESOLUTION OF CONGRESS, NOV. 3, 1814. *Exergue.* BATTLES OF CHIPPEWA, JULY 5, 1814; NIAGARA, JULY 25, 1814; ERIE, SEPT. 17, 1814. *Furst, F.* Size 40.

Miller's for the same, as follows :

Obverse. Bust of General Miller. *Legend.* BRIGADIER-GENERAL JAMES MILLER. *Exergue.* I'LL TRY. *Furst, F.*

Reverse. Two armies engaged upon a hill. One party is charging the other to obtain possession of a battery. On the plain below in the left background, a camp is seen with a body of men drawn up in reserve, and in the foreground is a park of artillery, drawn by four horses, with men riding on the trucks. *Legend.* RESOLUTION OF CONGRESS, NOV. 3, 1814. *Exergue.* BATTLES OF CHIPPEWA, JULY 5, 1814; NIAGARA, JULY 25, 1814; ERIE, SEPT. 17, 1814. *Furst, F.* Size 40.

Ripley's for the same has

Obverse. Head of General Ripley. *Legend.* BRIGADIER-GENERAL ELEAZER W. RIPLEY. *Furst, F.*

Reverse. Fame is represented hanging upon the branches of a palm tree, a tablet bearing the inscriptions CHIPPEWA, NIAGARA, ERIE. In her right hand, which hangs gracefully by her side, she carries her trumpet and a wreath of laurel, the latter encircling the former. *Legend.* RESOLUTION OF CONGRESS, NOV. 3, 1814. *Exergue.* BATTLES OF CHIPPEWA, JULY 5, 1814; NIAGARA, JULY 25, 1814; ERIE, AUG. 15, SEPT. 17, 1814. *Furst, F.* Size 40.

The seventh and last medal awarded under the resolve of the 3d November, 1814, was to General Alexander Macomb for his gallant conduct at the battle of Plattsburg, on the occasion of its attack by the English army, September 11, 1814.

Obverse. Bust of General Macomb. *Legend.* MAJOR-GENERAL ALEXANDER MACOMB. *Furst, F.*

Reverse. A view of the battle of Plattsburg. In the left background vessels of war are seen upon Lake Champlain in action, and beyond in the right background, mountains are visible. In the left foreground, troops are crossing a bridge, planted at the head of which is the American standard. Plattsburg in view to the left in flames. *Legend.* RESOLUTION OF CONGRESS, NOV. 3, 1814. *Exergue.* BATTLE OF PLATTSBURG, SEPT. 11, 1814. *Furst, F.* Size 40.

On the 8th of January, 1815, was fought the only battle on American soil the anniversary of which is sacredly remembered and rigidly celebrated all over the Union. Congress on the 27th of the following February, voted a gold medal to General Jackson for his brave and successful repulse of the enemy under General Sir Edward Packinham, in their attack upon New Orleans.

Obverse. Bust of General Jackson. *Legend.* MAJOR-GENERAL ANDREW JACKSON. *Furst, F.*

Reverse. Victory seated, and supporting a tablet before her with her left hand, which also holds a laurel wreath and from which has fallen a palm branch, has commenced recording the glorious victory of the 8th of January, and has headed the tablet with the word Orleans, but is interrupted by a female personifying Peace, who holds an olive branch in her right hand

and with her left points to the tablet, as if directing Victory to record the peace between the United States and Great Britain. Victory is in the act of turning round to listen to her instructions. *Legend.* RESOLUTION OF CONGRESS, FEB. 27, 1815. *Exergue.* BATTLE OF NEW ORLEANS, JANUARY, 8, 1815. *Furst, F.* Size 40.

I must revert once more to those sons of Neptune who upheld so valiantly the honor of our flag in the last war with England, and whose brave spirit has descended untarnished to their successors of the present day, and this time to record honor done to two citizens of Philadelphia, one still living and the hero of decidedly the most brilliant engagement of the war. Captain Charles Stewart, on the 20th of February, 1815, captured, after a most skillful combat lasting only forty minutes, the two British war vessels Cyane of 34 guns, and Levant of 21 guns, with the frigate Constitution, 52 guns. Considering the superior weight of the enemy's metal, and their forces being divided, this may be deemed the most noteworthy naval action of modern days. One year later, Congress on the 22d of February passed complimentary resolutions to Commodore Stewart and the officers and crew under his command, and ordered a gold medal to be presented to him, and silver ones to his officers, commemorative of the victory. By resolution of the same date, a gold medal was awarded to Captain James Biddle, for his capture of the English man-of-war Penguin, on the 23d of March, 1815. Silver ones were also in this instance presented to his commissioned officers.

Commodore Stewart's medal has

Obverse. Bust of Captain Stewart. *Legend.* CAROLUS STEWART NAVIS AMER. CONSTITUTION. DUX. *Furst, F.*

Reverse. View of the engagement taking place between the Constitution and the Cyane and Levant. The two latter occupy respectively the right and left foreground, and in the centre of the background between them, is the Constitution. *Legend.* UNA VICTORIAM ERIPUIT RATIBUS BINIS. *Exergue.* INTER CONSTITU. NAV. AMERI. ET LEVANT ET CYANE NAV. ANG. DIE XX FEBR., MDCCCXV. *Furst, F.* Size 40.

12

Commodore Biddle's.

Obverse. Head of Captain Biddle. *Legend.* THE CONGRESS OF THE UNITED STATES TO CAPTAIN JAMES BIDDLE. *Exergue.* FOR HIS GALLANTRY, GOOD CONDUCT, AND SERVICES. *Furst, F.*

Reverse. The engagement between the Hornet and the Penguin, in sight of the peak of Tristan d' Acunha ; the Penguin is very much injured in her upper rigging, her guns are silenced, and her colors are trailing in the water over her stern. *Legend.* CAPTURE OF THE BRITISH SHIP PENGUIN, BY THE UNITED STATES SHIP HORNET. *Exergue.* OFF TRISTAN D' ACUNHA, MARCH XXIII, MDCCCXV. *Furst, F.* Size 40.

Congress while awarding our commanders on the sea did not entirely overlook the just claims of the leaders of our land forces, for, although after some delay, they did justice to General William Henry Harrison and Governer Isaac Shelby for their distinguished victory over the combined English and Indian forces at the battle of the Thames, on the 5th of October, 1813. By resolution of April 4, 1818, gold medals were ordered to be presented to these two gentlemen, for the above last mentioned action.

The medal to President Harrison has on its

Obverse. Bust of General Harrison. *Legend.* MAJOR-GENERAL WILLIAM H. HARRISON. *Furst, F.*

Reverse. A female placing a wreath around two bayonets fixed on muskets, and a color staff stacked, over a drum and a cannon, a bow and a quiver ; with her right hand she holds a halberd and rests upon an American shield. From the point of union of the stack hangs a badge with the inscription, Fort Meigs, Battle of the Thames. *Legend.* RESOLUTION OF CONGRESS, APRIL 4, 1818. *Exergue.* BATTLE OF THE THAMES, OCTOBER 5, 1813. *Furst, F.* Size 40.

Governor Shelby's medal has

Obverse. Bust of Governor Shelby. *Legend.* GOVERNOR ISAAC SHELBY, *Furst, F.*

Reverse. The battle, with the Indian force drawn up upon the edge of the wood in the right background. On the left background the American troops have broken the Indian line, and on the left foreground a body of American infantry are seen advancing to the attack. In the foreground, on the right, Governor Shelby is charging the enemy at the head of his mounted rangers; and in the centre, on the open space between the opposing columns, the principal event of the action is represented—the death of the great Tecumseh at the hands of Colonel Richard M. Johnson, afterwards Vice-President of the United States. *Legend.* BATTLE OF THE THAMES, OCTOBER 5, 1813. *Exergue.* RESOLUTION OF CONGRESS, APRIL 4, 1818. *Furst, F.* Size 40.

I will close this notice of our National Medals which has spread under my pen to a much greater length than I at first intended or supposed, with the record that twenty-one years after the signing of the Treaty of Ghent, Congress was taken with one of those spasmodic affections by which sluggish bodies are sometimes singularly moved, and on the 13th of February, 1835, passed a vote awarding to Colonel George Croghan a gold medal for his gallant defence of Fort Sandusky, on the 2d of August, 1813, against the attack of a vastly superior force of five hundred British regulars and eight hundred Indians, commanded by General Proctor.

Obverse. Bust of Colonel Croghan. *Legend.* PRESENTED BY CONGRESS TO COLONEL GEORGE CROGHAN. *Exergue.* 1835. *Furst, F.*

Reverse. The fort of Sandusky with the enemy arranged in front, and the flag flying on the tower; on the bay in the background are seen three vessels. *Legend.* PARS MAGNA FUIT. *Exergue.* SANDUSKY, 2D: AUGUST, 1813. *Furst, F.* Size 40.

I hope the gentlemen who have so kindly been my audience during the reading of this dry compilation of facts, and imperfect descriptions of the only monuments erected in honor of the great battles of our country, both on sea and on land, and of their heroes, will see the propriety of urging upon the Federal Government their attention to the correction of our coinage, somewhat on the plan laid before them in the petition of this Society, presented by our Honorary Vice-President, Mr. Johnson, at the last session of Congress, so that our coinage may become the repository of the country's history, and then when the avenging hand of time has swept into eternity all other records, these little pieces of metal may become to future ages what the coins of ancient Greece and Rome are to us, the historians of the long forgotten past.

www.ingramcontent.com/pod-product-compliance
Lightning Source LLC
Chambersburg PA
CBHW020555270326

41927CB00006B/852